ENTERPRISE FITNESS

4/25/09

Gary,
Thank you for your help
on This. you are a
great professor (still) and
friend.

Jo

ENTERPRISE FITNESS

John Covington

TATE PUBLISHING & *Enterprises*

Published by Tate Publishing & Enterprises, LLC
127 E. Trade Center Terrace | Mustang, Oklahoma 73064 USA
1.888.361.9473 | www.tatepublishing.com

Tate Publishing is committed to excellence in the publishing industry. The company reflects the philosophy established by the founders, based on Psalm 68:11,
"The Lord gave the word and great was the company of those who published it."

Book design copyright © 2009 by Tate Publishing, LLC. All rights reserved.
Cover design by Jeff Fisher
Interior design by Nathan Harmony

Published in the United States of America

ISBN: 978-1-60799-431-2
1. Business & Economics: Leadership
2. Business & Economics: Organizational Behavior
09.06.11

Table of Contents

Foreword

I met John Covington as a peer member of the Leadership Board for the College of Engineering at the University of Alabama. At one of the board retreats in Destin, Florida, I *really* got to know John minutes after he came face to face with a panther during a bike ride. From the look (astonished) and color (red) of his face, I was concerned that John was on the verge of a major heat stroke. After he related the up close and personal meeting of Mr. Panther, I had a much better understanding of what his "look" was trying to convey.

Since that day, John has become a close personal friend and professional associate. As an entrepreneur with four start-ups (SEAKO, TXEN, DAXKO, Yacht Record) under my belt, I appreciate the message that John's spirited and humorous writing brings to those of us with engineering or technical backgrounds. My first encounter with one of John's books (*Lets Don't Pave the Cow Paths*) helped me when I was struggling to escape from a business venture that was ill conceived. His clear, earthy tales of woe from his own experiences had me laughing and his weaving of Christian faith in his writing was most appropriate as I struggled with difficult decisions.

In his latest book, *Enterprise Fitness*, John hits a home run as he continues to relate, in an often funny way, how we must continuously look at the culture of our businesses if we are to be willing to disrupt our business processes to bring about change and renewal with new alignments. Over the years, I have read many books on management (a word that I disdain), business organization (if it needs organization, it is too big), and leadership (better to lead than push) as I have tried to improve my own leadership skills. What I like about John's approach to these subjects is that he is real in his writing as he chronicles his path through forty years of manufacturing experience and his encounters with real people that he worked for, with, and over.

As I read the final pages of *Enterprise Fitness*, John's writing and weaving of Paul's words to the Corinthians (12:4–26) took me back to my high school chemistry class in 1959. My high school chemistry teacher, Dr. J. O. Davie, could make the most complex subject come alive with his graphic portrayals and experiments of what happens when we pour sugar in gasoline, hold either but not both sides of 120 volt extension cords, and gently hammer a rubber stopper into a brimming bottle of water. In a like manner, John takes us on a journey, making sure that we constantly and continuously disrupt and improve our business processes, while holding up, through respect and love, each person in our companies—just as Paul did in his writings to the Corinthians.

—Tom Patterson
Chairman of the Board of DAXKO and Yacht Records

Preface

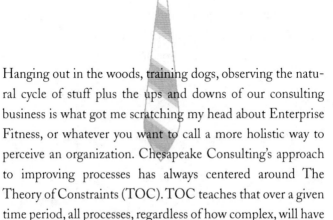

Hanging out in the woods, training dogs, observing the natural cycle of stuff plus the ups and downs of our consulting business is what got me scratching my head about Enterprise Fitness, or whatever you want to call a more holistic way to perceive an organization. Chesapeake Consulting's approach to improving processes has always centered around The Theory of Constraints (TOC). TOC teaches that over a given time period, all processes, regardless of how complex, will have very few elements that determine their capacity relative to their goal or reason for being. If you can find that element, then you can make a quick and powerful impact on the output of the process. This makes for very happy people.

I hope *Enterprise Fitness* adds to your understanding of yourself, your organization, and how you might become more effective. I really do mean the "adds to" part. There are many wonderful books, lectures, approaches, and experiences that all add to our development, and no one is best. I love reading books from all of the management "gurus"; however, I get turned off by some of their egos and those that imply that they have invented water and air.

Leadership principles have been around since the beginning of time. As humans, we need to dive in and struggle with what has already been taught and already exists. I have found great books of wisdom to be the most inspiring and useful resource. If a particular guru is on the money, then their teaching will be in alignment with what has already been taught and their value is to deepen learning. That better understanding of something that already exists is their noble endeavor, and thank heavens for their efforts.

When I hear a *new* approach to leadership or improvement, I listen to see how the language differs and how they are in alignment with existing wisdom. If they claim something new, then they probably do not know enough to know what they don't know. My friend, and one of the wise guru's, Dr. Eli Goldratt, once said that if something is valid, others are talking about it but in a different manner.

There are several points that I want to emphasize in this book:

1. The quality of your organizational culture is critical. In the long run it determines how successful you will be. I know that sounds obvious, but it has been my experience that most companies do not proactively address culture.

2. Culture is an effect. It is an effect of clarity of purpose and the quality of leadership. At times you may feel you are reading a book on process improvement, and at other times you may feel you are reading about human relationships. My intent is to link the two and highlight their interdependency.

3.   Both clarity of purpose and quality of leadership are areas in which all of us can make improvements by engaging some common sense practices. What that means is that we can all take specific actions to improve our working culture, thus improve our long-term chances of success.

I will make reference to scriptures from the Holy Bible. I embrace Christianity, so the Holy Bible is my preferred book of wisdom, and it is the one with which I am most familiar.

In the editing process of this book I have had many friends and colleagues comment, and I value their input. Without their input and help, I would never be able to publish a book. On *Enterprise Fitness*, I have gotten varied opinions on how much *religion* to put in the book. How far do I push the envelope before the value to the reader is hurt or I lose readers that do not share my chosen path to spiritual fulfillment? I would not attempt to write this book if I did not want to enhance the understanding and practical application of principles that I feel are universal in their nature, regardless of the approach you take for your own faith journey.

What I am learning is that life, and everything in life, has natural patterns and, there are some cause and effect relationships. If we begin to develop an understanding of these patterns and interconnections, then we might end up being better and more effective playmates for those with whom we spend our time. To leave God out of this discussion, for me, would limit our learning. I am going to roll the dice on this and promise to be as thoughtful as I can be on how I use my particular faith to illustrate important principles.

So, let's begin this trip through *Enterprise Fitness*.

Chapter 1
That Culture Thing

Have you ever walked into a store or plant and gotten *that feel*? It could be good or bad; enjoyable or uncomfortable; relaxed or stressful. Dr. Meg Wheatley mentions this in her book *Leadership and the New Science* and maintains that this *feel* is the combination of purpose, relationships, and information. I think she is right.

What is a bad culture? Until I asked myself that question while writing this book, I had never given it much thought. Is it just one of those things that you sort of know it when you see or feel it? I don't know. I asked my colleagues, who are experienced leaders from a variety of industries and settings, to give me some feedback, and here is some of what they had to say:

> The goal of the organization is not the highest priority of the members. Usually power and prestige are. The consequences of doing the wrong thing are loss of power and prestige. Information does not flow or communication of vital information is not freely available; it is rationed out. Information is used as a source of power. Improvements are slow if existent. Changes that members can be held

Enterprise Fitness

accountable for are dangerous. Much emphasis is given to badges of power, organizational charts, titles, office locations, furniture, and access to members at higher levels of the organization.

—Carl Gerhiser

An unhealthy culture is bound together by unhealthy relationships and values. Fear, greed, and domination come to mind. An example of a poor culture is the company which was so dysfunctional that a suicide was committed on the shop floor. Its characteristics were poor communication, unfocused leadership, lack of trust, relationships that were characterized by *getting away* with illegal or unethical actions, sneaking around, being dishonest. Without a clear compass of good (healthy) values and relationships, the bond became one of "see what we can get away with.

—Dr. Penny Gladwell.

To give an example of bad culture, at one of my duty stations we had two weeks to act on incoming correspondence. Since I was not busy, I would complete mine the day I received something. Exactly two weeks later, my supervisor would ask me where my response was. I would dig it out of his inbox; he would initial it (usually without reading it) and send it on. Why two weeks? Because that is when the item would show up on the delinquent correspondence list.

—Joe Closs

To me, a bad culture is an organization where people are afraid of doing the wrong thing.

—Jim Turbok

Bad culture is one where workers are stifled by fear. Fear of being disrespected, being publicly reprimanded should they make a mistake, speaking up, retribution should they disagree with their supervisor, and fear of failure.

—Saundra Barrett

The best indication of corporate culture is found where the rubber meets the road, not the board room. Watch the engineers and supervisors as they walk the floor. Is their head up and are they walking at a brisk pace? Do you see them having a positive conversation about the daily issues? Do the operators turn to you with a positive attitude as you pass or do they simply stand there with their head down?

—Brad Newman

Here are some of the other things we have seen in *challenged* cultures:

- People not willing to talk openly. I have been places where upper management has instructed their employees not to cooperate with the consulting firm.
- People talking about people instead of ideas, strategies, issues, and business.
- A lack of humor.
- Obsession with cost vs. growth.

Culture is what it is. When you walk into an organization it is there—good, bad, or so-so. It exists and the level of *goodness* determines how well the organization accomplishes the purpose in the long run. It has been my experience that most organizations go through ups and downs with respect to culture. I know my business has.

At one time, I used to think you had to have a good culture to make money. I was wrong. I used to run a facility for Sherwin-Williams. People that were fired were referred to as "being shot." Good people were shot at such an alarming rate that it was quite flippant. Needless to say, there was a lot of fear and distrust at the company. However, S&W was extremely successful, and their CEO, Jack Breen, was held in high esteem by many. But good culture releases the discretionary energy/effort of an organization. Somehow I cannot help but think that performance of S&W would have been even better had Mr. Breen won over the hearts of his employees and released that energy and effort. However, he is the fellow that turned around a dying Fortune 200 Company and made it successful, not me.

Trust

At what level do people trust one another? Of all the issues, one is key—trust. Trust is an indication of the quality of relationships, and if we embrace Dr. Wheatley's model, that actually makes some sense. If I look back on my experiences, I see lack of trust as a common denominator in bad cultures and the reverse to be true in good cultures.

Dr. Wheatley said that systems are held together by purpose, relationships, and information. I think we can assume that information flows through relationships. That gives us two things to focus on—purpose and relationships, and the key component of relationships is trust.

Trust is very powerful and can overcome bias and other prejudices over time. Trust must be earned, and unfortunately trust that has been earned over years can be destroyed in one act of betrayal. I am certain we have all been on both ends of that scenario.

Trust is always a choice, so it is something we can control, and most times it involves us letting go of control. Let me give a few examples.

I have a young German Shepard, and she and I are going through some intensive training together. Part of this training is tracking. Without the dog, I make a trail by walking around in a grassy field and bring the dog out later to follow the scent (they actually smell the crushed grass where you have stepped). Early in our training, I thought Maggie was headed in the wrong direction, so I corrected her. Our instructor quickly corrected me and said, "Trust your dog, John. Trust your dog." Of course, Maggie was correct, and fortunately she was confident enough in her ability to keep going in the right direction. As we progress, Maggie will make more and more of the decisions as to where we go, and I will just have to trust her.

The Bible is full of stories of trust. In Genesis 6:14, God tells Noah, "So make yourself an ark of cypress wood; make rooms in it and coat it with pitch inside and out." God then gets into the details of how big this thing is supposed to be. "Say again! You want me to do what? You have got to be kidding," would probably have been my response. Thank heavens Noah was a tad more trusting.

In Genesis 12:1, God says to Abram, "Leave your country, your people and your father's household and go into the land I will show you." Again, my response would probably have been along the lines of, "What? You want me to just pick up and leave with no job, no plan, and not knowing where I am going?"

Trust and faith are almost tied together. We trust and have faith in our doctors and dentists to do their job and make us well. This is an interesting type of trust. Do we have much choice? My tooth hurts; it is beyond the point of taking a pain reliever, and I do not know how to fix it. I must trust a dentist, I have no choice.

However, work is different. Do I trust that new consultant to facilitate a workshop with a big account? At what point can you let go?

Early in my career I worked for Stauffer Chemicals, which was a company that trusted young engineers with an enormous level of responsibility. I remember one of their executives telling me that they knew there were going to be some mistakes but the benefit of developing all that young talent was worth the risk. Prior to Stauffer I had worked for DuPont, where I learned a lot but did not get to do a lot or gain much hands-on experience. I accomplished and learned more at Stauffer, since they trusted me with several large projects and leadership responsibility.

Trust is the key element in effective delegation. If I delegate something to you and then micro-manage it, I would probably be better off doing it myself. The problem with that is that something else would not get done. To leverage your leadership influence, you must choose to trust.

When you proactively trust people, it will normally be a

rewarding experience. We have many people at Chesapeake that have been loyal to our company and to me for years. We trust one another; it is the way we work well together. However, when you trust, you will occasionally get burned. I have been hurt emotionally and financially by people that have betrayed my trust. That is part of the deal, and it is going to happen. If we dwell on those that did not prove to be trustworthy, then we begin to limit our ability to trust again, and that would be terrible.

Trust is an ongoing, tough assignment—and may be the most important assignment with respect to growing as a leader. It is a day-to-day issue since there is not a *finite* amount of trust. Your words, but most of all your behavior, speak volumes on how much you trust someone. It is a mental exercise that you control.

I have spent a lot of time on trust because it is the key ingredient in relationships and those relationships are the key ingredients in the culture we are trying to build.

Chapter 2
The Problem

What do we need to do to improve our work cultures? A process of ongoing improvement can only take place in a work culture that is accepting of change.

When I ask people that run organizations about their problems, they tell us that half of their issues are process related and half people. If we make the valid assumption that most people are pretty good, then the problem is with the cultures we have created. The good news is we can make a positive impact on our cultures, and we can do it by embracing some common sense principles that have been around for centuries.

We want to learn to trust and honor our people more. And we want to insure that our purpose and the processes to achieve our purpose are crystal clear. If we successfully do those two things along with ongoing education and information flow, our cultures will snap into fine shape.

All is Well

When I began our consulting business, I was blessed with some very good first accounts. The Lord really does look out for dummies, and I needed all the help I could get. The following are some examples of the different business I worked with my first years: some were successes and some were not. What was the difference and how could I effect a change so that every client was a success? I knew this difference would be the key to success.

Frank Trotta was the vice president of global operations for Rohm & Haas Plastic Additives Division. His right hand assistant in charge of plant improvement was Bob Halter. I had met Bob at a theory of constraints seminar in Atlanta, thus he was on our propaganda mailing list. Our marketing efforts of phone calls and mailings had finally paid off, and Bob wanted to meet with us in Philadelphia, which was their corporate headquarters.

Bob, Frank, and I had something in common; we are all chemical engineers. Chemical engineers across the country are almost like a fraternity. It is a curriculum that resides in the college of engineering but hangs somewhere in space between arts and science and engineering. The chemistry professors always hated us because we made more money than chemists. The engineering departments didn't quite believe we were *real* engineers and looked upon us as glorified plumbers. Since no one else liked us, we always bonded with one another, regardless of where we went to school. As an Alabama grad, I even like Auburn Chemical Engineers since being a chemical engineer trumps the fact they are Auburn fans.

The Philadelphia meeting went well and the sales process

moved to the next phase, a trip to their plant in Louisville, Kentucky. The implementations went well at Louisville and then at their Bristol, Pennsylvania plant. These facilities realized huge increases in production, and the Rohm & Haas employees that were part of the implementation with us were leading the efforts after we left. All of our projects go through a series of events—assessment, education, design/ plan, and then implementation.

In the assessment phase, our consultants get a rough feel for where the facility is today and what their potential is based on their constraint operations. We identify a client implementation team consisting of people closest to the work. The team goes through some education together where they learn new ways to move things through their process. They then develop a specific plan for their facility, and we execute the plan and monitor results. There has always been a lot of people interaction, but our approach was heavy on the process improvement side of the equation.

It was almost too easy. The customer was ecstatic and so were we. We collected our fees for those plants, and Rohm & Haas rewarded us with numerous other plants and opportunities. Gosh, this consulting stuff was pretty cool.

The collecting our fees part is important. One of the ways we price is *fixed price; fixed deliverable.* After an initial assessment, we figure the value of the service based on what we feel we can put on the bottom line and then estimate resources to achieve the results. If all goes really well and we get done early (client is getting results and has taken over), then we come out better than expected. If things do not go as well, we spend more time, which limits our ability to take on additional projects. Having some level of predictability is important to us.

For large projects, we do not want to price by the day or hour. If we priced that way, it gives us an incentive to stay there forever whether we get results or not. We feel that does not serve the customer well nor does it meet our needs.

Another *too easy* account was Stanley Furniture. I first met the Stanley folks at a two- day workshop I was giving at Patrick Henry Community College in Martinsville, Virginia. There were other furniture companies there as well, but the Stanley folks were different. Whereas the other furniture people were intent on telling me why what I was saying would not work in the furniture industry, Stanley actually appeared to be listening and asking some excellent questions. They had a large group of people at the workshop, including the chairman of the board, Albert Prillaman, and their executive vice president, Larry Webb. After the workshop, Stanley executives invited me to their facility and we began a relationship that lasted several years.

Stanley leapfrogged the industry in service, quality, inventory turns, and profits. However, to achieve those results they had to totally rethink the way they did business, the way they measured results, and the way they looked upon their financial reports. It was a change to the point that it even affected their banking relationships. The people at Stanley moved way outside their comfort zone to achieve remarkable performance. To move that far away from your traditional way of doing business takes a lot of courage and a huge leap of faith. When I look back, I am humbled that they asked us to help provide leadership on that journey. Ten years later,

Albert Prillaman asked me back and said, "John, you gave us a good ten year run. We now need for you to come up with some ideas to take us ten more years as other people are starting to catch up."

The relationship with Rohm & Haas and Stanley Furniture was very profitable for them and for us. Both of these companies had wonderful cultures. They had excellent leadership that was engaged and they were clear about who they were and what was expected. We worked together, got results, then went on to another account and they continued to mint money. At one time, we helped Clemson University and later North Carolina State host manufacturing productivity workshops where we would have our customers come and present case studies. Bob Summerhays of Rohm & Haas gave such a presentation several times for us. In response to a question, I recall Bob telling the audience that one of their plants paid out their investment in Chesapeake's services in less than two weeks of increased production. I cringed. I wanted our customers to get a good value, but it was obvious we under priced that particular assignment.

They are All Not Perfect

After twenty years of being in business, I can count on one hand the number of *failures* we have had with respect to projects. Even one or two that I would count as failures, the customers to this day feel they got their money's worth. We have found that all customers are not created equal. We go into some companies and get excellent results in a reasonable period of time. In those cases everyone is happy. In other situations we would struggle for two or three times as long to get the same impact. The customer may be happy, but it costs us money because we could not use our resources to begin another project. This problem was always a key topic at our planning meetings. We could take the same consultants, the same tried-and-true approach, and the same material and get drastically different results. The only apparent variable was the culture of the client's company.

We had a choice. We could test for and only work with companies that had excellent cultures, or we could begin to address the cultural issues (the soft side, as some folks call it) of our customers. We joked that if we chose only to work with companies that had great cultures, then we would certainly narrow our market opportunities.

I will not name companies we feel struggled culturally, but we will highlight some we feel did a lot of things right. Now, if you are one of our customers and I do not mention your name as being real nice, that does not mean you are one of the difficult ones. What it means is that I have enough *good* examples. Anyway, the vast majority of folks we have worked with since 1988 have been super—different degrees of super, but super nevertheless.

Those slower accounts were costing us money. One particular customer was in the transportation industry and was a tier one supplier. You would immediately recognize their name. They produced an assembled product, and their problem was that they were not getting enough production out the door. One of their customers produced very large and expensive heavy-duty construction equipment. This company had millions and millions of dollars of work-in-process inventory that was ready to ship if only they had the part they purchased from our client. The pressure was on to get those parts shipped where their customer could ship products and improve cash flow.

There were six departments in the factory; assembly and five departments that produced components that fed assembly. The constraint of the entire company was one of the component areas. We had developed a plan to increase capacity for that small part of the plant by adding nine people. There were probably five hundred employees at this plant, and by adding nine people the output would increase by nearly twenty percent and all of that volume was sold. Those are huge numbers, and profits would soar if they would execute the plan.

There was some resistance to hiring people since the plant had been in a cost-cutting mentality for years. Several weeks went by and the head of the department had not hired anyone, much less nine people. By the way, this was no longer a *suggestion*; the plant manager had ordered that the nine people be hired.

Too much time was going by, and the company was not getting the results expected. I recall attending one of the daily production meetings, where there was a lot of yammering about this and that, but I had not heard the important information so I asked the question; "How much product did we ship out yesterday?" There was dead silence and no one knew. I waited for an answer. Finally, one lady spoke up and said, "I could go back to my office and get that data." More silence. She finally got up and went and got the information, which I felt was the most significant information for them at this time. Their plant had plenty of data—charts everywhere and they appeared to measure everything—but no one in that meeting knew how much product they had produced.

The production numbers were horrible. There was no way they would ever catch up going at the current rate. We began to dive into the details, and sure enough, the same component area was starving assembly. I asked, "Have you hired the nine additional employees?" The head of the area sort of gave me a smirk. I wanted to whack him upside the head. It was a clear-cut case of insubordination. The plant manager was not even in the meeting. He was uninvolved in the most import issue that faced his facility and did not provide good leadership. His attitude was reflected in the plant culture. The company had wasted at least a month due to not executing a simple instruction. The plan was finally executed and results were obtained. However, it took us twice as long as it should have. That cost our company money.

We sold the same company a project in one of their plants in Great Britain, and part of our fees were at risk based on productivity increases. Our people voiced a concern about their company leadership and whether or not they could execute. Our fears of poor leadership were realized, and it cost our company a fortune. A problem account just down the road is bad. A problem account across the Atlantic is a disaster.

There was no doubt—we had good accounts where we made money and got a lot of satisfaction, and we had bad accounts where we spent more time than needed. We had a business problem.

What is the Issue?

Many of those in our company are geeky engineering types. We are very boring and analyze the crap out of everything. Why do we have excellent results with company A and it takes us twice as long (or longer) with company B? Why? We looked at each account and situation. The consultants, the material, and the approach were consistent. The only variable was the culture of where we were working. So we had several decisions to make.

Do we only work with companies that have good cultures and have a high probability of success? That is a possibility because we get a good feel for culture during the assessment phase. However, that does limit the market some. In fact, it limited the market a whole lot since almost everyone we work with has some key culture issues that impede improvement. We figured this was not a good approach.

Do we increase the price for companies we feel are going to be a problem? That was an interesting question. The logical answer to that one would be yes. However, that would almost do the same as the first option. Twenty years in business has taught me that the company that squabbles over price is going to be a problem down the road. Those companies that understand that they are dealing with huge profit increases do not blink an eye at a fair price for our service. When someone starts to nickel and dime me, I know I am in trouble because that same company probably thinks they already know it all and are unwilling to make a change. They are actually the companies that need us the most.

A last option would be to develop products and services that would address the culture issue. So that is what we chose. We are happy with that decision because now the organizations that we engage that have some culture issues benefit even more from a relationship with our company.

The Parable of the Sower

I think one of the best stories on how dependent we are on culture is the one Jesus told and explained in Matthew 13:1–9, 18–23. I will paraphrase the story. There was a farmer out sowing seeds. Some fell on the path, and birds came along and ate them. Some fell in rocky places where there was not much soil. The plants grew quickly, but because it was shallow they wilted as soon as the sun came up. Other seeds fell among the thorns and weeds and were choked out. Today, the thorns and weeds could be all of the unimportant things that consume our time at work. And some fell in good soil, grew, and yielded fruit. Of course, what we are looking for in our organizations is more fruit. Let the soil represent our organizational culture. The different types of soil, rocks, rocky soil, weedy areas, and deep fertile soil, all can represent the state or our organizations when we sow seeds of change.

We know of a large company that is implementing a very detailed and sophisticated improvement process in all of their plants. We did a leadership and culture assessment of one of the facilities where they are beginning to implement the change and found the leadership team to be dysfunctional and the culture not ready for these new seeds that are supposed to yield additional fruit in the form of profits. This scenario will not have a happy ending. It will take more company resources to install the change, and there is a huge risk that the change will not be embedded in the culture. As soon as the consultants leave the plant, they will more than likely snap right back into the way they were doing things in the past, and the company will have wasted their money. When we asked the corporate leadership why they picked that plant, they answered, "It was one of the plants with the most need." Our thoughts are that the reason it had such a poor performance is because of the poor soil. The company would have been better off working on the soil before sowing expensive seeds of change.

Several years ago, I saw a statistic that over 75 percent of change efforts fail. That darn culture thing is something we are going to need to address.

Chapter 3

Transformation and Flow (And the Way You Achieve Purpose)

Every organization has a purpose, and to achieve its purpose, there are processes involved. In order to clearly understand *purpose*, one must clearly understand the process employed to create the purpose. Your organization transforms something from one state to another through process(es).

Let's say you run a furniture business. You take lumber, hardware, glue, and other raw materials that are relatively worthless to a homeowner and transform them into a fine suite of furniture that sells for two thousand dollars. In order to do this, you go through a set of dependent steps. The wood must go through the kiln before it goes to a dimension mill, then to machining operations, and ultimately assembly and finishing. Each of these steps has issues of capacity (how much can I get through in a day) and variability.

If you are a drug company, you might transform an idea into a molecule that is approved and cures some illness. A college transforms someone from one state of knowledge to another. A sales department transforms a prospect into a customer.

In transformation and flow there are four issues involved:

1. Dependency—What are the steps involved and how must they be sequenced?

2. Capacity—How much can an operation produce? Later on, we will learn that the lowest capacity operation is the one that is critical.

3. Variability—How much fluctuation is involved?

4. Inventory—How much stored capacity is available?

All organizational systems and their parts have these elements, and that is how they achieve their stated purpose.

Let me give some examples:

The United Methodist Church (UMC)

We may as well start off with one of the most bizarre accounts for a manufacturing focused consulting firm.

Our work with the UMC began in the early 1990s when Ezra Earl Jones, one of their leaders, had some interest in the Theory of Constraints. After some visits, seminars, and retreats, we had a twelve-day strategic planning session with several of their bishops and other leaders. Their stated purpose is, "To make disciples." When you mention *make* to an engineer, they think manufacturing process, drawings, and all sorts of cool things. So, we divided the leaders up into teams and told them to go off and draw their process.

Can you imagine what you would get if you ask a bunch of religious leaders to go off and draw a process? Many of these good folks are very arts and crafts oriented and can actually sing well enough so dogs don't howl. However, process drawings are not the first thing that pops into their mind. So we had to do some adapting.

The drawing I remember the most was one from the group headed by Bishop Sharon Brown Christopher. During their presentation, they showed a view of the church from an observer looking down on earth from outer space. They had *dim souls* flowing into the church and much lighter souls coming out the back of the church. These souls re-circulated back into the church and brought some more dim souls with them. Bishop Christopher said that if the church were doing its job, the world would continue to get brighter and brighter. Wow, how cool was that? I do not think an engineer could have done any better.

I then asked the Bishop and her team, "What is in the box you have drawn as the church? What steps are involved in making these disciples?" The group had pondered that question before, so it was not long before they came up with four steps:

1. People are *invited* into the box

2. They *relate* to God and to one another.

3. That relationship is *nurtured* through Bible study, prayer, and small groups.

4. They are *sent out* into the world to do good things, like address injustice and participate in acts of mercy and mis-

sion work and tell other people their story on how God is working in their life.

Again, I thought that was pretty cool for a bunch of non-engineers to come up with process steps to create something as intangible as a disciple.

I wanted them to dig a little deeper. We had given them some basic education in the theory of constraints. "So, of those four steps in your process, where is the constraint?"

The bishops and other leaders did not even hesitate, "Relating to God and one another," was their response. They said that in nine out of ten churches that is where the constraint was located. I was taken back by the speed and certainty of their answer.

"So, how does the process of relating to God and one another work?" I asked.

There was much conversation, but the common denominator, and what came out, was the need for a spiritual leader. It seemed as though the concept of spiritual leader was emerging as the constraint for the entire United Methodist Church; and I would suspect that would be the case with all churches.

"Okay, if I were walking through your factory and happened to trip over a spiritual leader, what would it look like? Since this is your precious and most valuable resource, we probably ought to know what it looks like."

They pondered for awhile and then came up with one who:

- Worships joyfully
- Is in prayer and meditation on a daily basis

- Is in Bible study and small group interaction
- Connects with other believers and develops meaningful relationships
- Shares their story with others

I have heard this same description from many church leaders and theologians, and for many it is the description of a disciple. I had an instructor in a lay leadership class tell us, "Disciples make disciples and members make members." This group of leaders was coming to the same conclusion. So, the machine that plays an integral part in making a disciple is a disciple.

One of the first issues they had is the realization that they were paying a whole lot of people to be spiritual leaders that did not meet those criteria. We learned that the Methodist Church signs up about one thousand new ministers per year, and they come from about fourteen universities, ranging in philosophy from somewhere to the right of Attila the Hun to somewhat to the left of the communist party. Contrast this to the U.S. Navy that pumps about one thousand new officers per year out of Annapolis with a much higher level of consistency in training.

However, the process for bringing on new pastors was not the issue. The main issue is how do they best utilize the ones they have? How best do we use this resource?

After much pondering, they came to the conclusion that the spiritual leaders in the Methodist Church should be on "the path" together. They defined the path as being the means of grace as described by their founder, John Wesley. They defined the means of grace as:

1. Worshiping regularly.

2. Observing the sacraments

3. Fasting

4. Daily prayer, study, and meditation

5. Conferencing with others on how God is working in your life.

6. Performing acts of mercy

7. Performing acts of justice

Their plan was for the bishops to be on the path with their direct reports and take that all the way down to the individual church member. It was a pretty cool plan which unfortunately they did not immediately execute. For whatever reason, these leaders defined their mission, defined the processes that cause the purpose to be realized, defined the constraint in the process (laser focus), but could not execute.

Why? Had serving their institution taken priority over serving the mission for which the institution was formed?

Rohm & Haas, Scotland

One of my all-time favorite accounts is Rohm & Haas. I enjoy spending some time in chemical plants, although I would no longer want to work in one. At 3 a.m., these places are alive and very, very well lit. From a distance at night, it is what a science fiction futuristic city might look like. There are special odors and sounds. In the seventies, most instruments in the industry were pneumatic, so there was the constant dull roar of compressors in the background and the hissing of escaping high-pressure air, steam, or inert gas. Some of the best cooks on the planet dwell in the control rooms and shops of chemical plants, and they ply their skills during off shifts. Chemical plants also have big toys; reactors, dryers, silos, distillation columns, and a variety of other cool things. I worked in a plant that had the world's largest vertical centrifuge. How about that?

This particular plant in Scotland transformed monomers to a plastic additive. The process had about the same number of steps as the disciple making process, but the steps are less complicated. Those human being constraints can be a real nightmare.

To make plastic additives, the monomer, along with some other raw materials, were added to a chemical reactor. This was a batch reactor and is not unlike cooking a stew at home. All the ingredients are added, then it cooks and reacts for awhile until the desired emulsion is created. The emulsion is then pumped to a large storage tank. From the storage tank, the material is pumped to a dryer where the liquid is driven off, leaving a fine powder. This material is then packaged in bags or tote sacks for shipment.

Our mission was to help the facility get more products shipped without adding additional capital.

The maximum output of the resource with the least capacity is the capacity of the entire system. I know that sounds obvious. However, as obvious as it seems, that is not how most people run their organizations. The disadvantage of not running your organization like this is that you do not have laser focus. At Rohm & Haas Scotland the constraint of the system was the reactors; however, most of their management effort and attention was on their dryers. In order to solve this problem, the people at Rohm & Haas needed to change their perspective and see their plant like we saw their plant. Otherwise, there would be no change.

The good people of R&H already had a way they ran the plant, and it was deeply embedded in the way they saw the world. Part of our improvement process is to give the customer some simple simulations that use the principles of flow we embrace. Once they have gained success using a simulated environment, we then, as a team, focus on their environment. The R&H folks discovered for themselves that the reactors were their constraint and determined how much output the plant could yield. It was not important what the dryers did as long as they did not slow down the reactors.

As we progressed, the entire facility understood that their goal was to produce more reactor batches per day, and everyone would be held accountable for that, not just those working in the reactor department. By everyone being held accountable, the different members of the organization underscored how they are all interdependent.

We began posting the number of reactor batches we produced the previous day at the entrance gate to the plant for all to see. Everyone delighted when the number went up and they could see that graph climbing. That is one of the thrills of manufacturing; you can measure your progress each day.

The unified purpose (more reactor batches) began to pull the team together. Instead of working as a dryer department or as a reactor department, they began working as a single unit with a single and very clear purpose of how to work together to achieve that purpose. The chief operator of the reactor section and the chief operator of the dryer section had worked in the same control room for many years. They commented to me that since they started focusing on the number of reactor batches produced per day, it was the first time they had actually seen how they were interconnected.

Within a couple of months, a new world had been created, and the plant achieved great results. Based on this project, this facility even won a corporate award for excellence.

So, they executed and were very successful. They had an excellent plant and corporate culture and had that "good feel."

Stanley Furniture

When we began working with Stanley, they operated like a typical furniture company. They had long runs of product to improve efficiency (or so they thought). Policies like this resulted in lots of inventory, missed shipments, high reject rates, missing parts at assembly, and a host of other evil things.

Stanley transforms lumber that looks sort of ugly into fine looking furniture. It is somewhat of a complex manufacturing system; hundreds and hundreds of parts must show up at the same time to be assembled. At the time we began working with them, they had five basic plants in one; a dimension mill that made the initial cuts of the wood, a chair plant, a table plant, a case plant, and a finishing plant. The case plant made china cabinets and fancy pieces that you would store your nice keepsakes in.

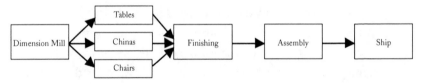

Figure 1 Stanley Manufacturing Process

Each of these plants operated almost independently. The entire plant complex did not get full accounting credit for an item until it was finished and approved to put in the warehouse. Since the nice Chinas had the most value, from a cost accounting standpoint, they were the first things produced that month. Then chairs and then tables. With about a week left in each month, the company realized that it had not shipped anything and disaster loomed. The problem was customers do not buy china cabinets, tables, and chairs. They buy suites of furniture, which is an assembled product consisting of matching chairs, tables, and china cabinets. That was somewhat of a paradigm shift and thought change for Stanley.

This change in mindset made logistics easier. Now one could look at the entire complex as one plant versus five. This made scheduling a lot easier. They simply scheduled the case clamp since each suite of furniture had some sort of case, and then released all material to the drumbeat of that piece of equipment. That meant that the proper tables, chairs, and cases all showed up to finishing and assembly at about the same time. This had a major positive impact on due date performance, inventory, cash flow, and many other business measures. However, more significantly, it caused a major shift in the way people worked and looked upon the company. In the initial phases of the implementation, it even strained banking relations because all of the consumed excess inventory showed up as an operating loss. The bank was happy with all the increased cash but could not understand the loss of funny money. Sometimes bankers are not very bright. (I assure you, our banker will not get a copy of this book.)

As I mentioned earlier, Stanley executed and led the industry for over a decade. Guess what they had in common with Rohm & Haas—that great culture. More than any furniture company that we have been associated with, Stanley placed a high value on corporate culture and trust.

Prior to beginning the improvement process, Stanley pledged to their employees that there would be no layoffs as a result of productivity increases. All savings would be through natural attrition. After that pledge was made and improvement was realized, the country went into a recession and there was pressure on the Stanley executives to have a layoff. They honored their word and did not have a layoff. Those are the types of actions that strengthen trust and culture.

Several Apparel Companies

We once worked with several apparel companies that I will lump into the same example; they were very similar. The problem they were having was high cost, high inventory, high waste, long lead times, and low service level. Other than that they were all doing pretty good.

These apparel operations were "cut and sew" facilities, and there was one operation in their process that was slower than another. In each case, if we took their slowest operation and calculated how much volume they would produce if they ran it very efficiently on the correct product, their outputs would go up twenty-five to forty percent. If you can increase output by that amount and not hire any additional people, you just hit a homerun, because cost per unit will plummet and service will soar. All of that translates to lots and lots of money.

This would involve operating more in a continuous flow mode versus moving large bundles of fabric through the plant. It was a difficult transition for both management and hourly employees, and the facilities we worked with did not make the change. Many of them lived and eventually died with a progressive bundle system and paying by piece rate. The manner in which we were suggesting they operate was so foreign to their traditional way that they could/would not make the shift. All of these companies had autocratic and patriarchal leadership styles that were reflected in their corporate culture.

In contrast, we had several apparel companies change their operation and do very well, as did Eric Scott Leather in Ste. Genevieve, Missouri.

GKN Automotive

An important part of any analysis and improvement effort is to properly define the system. GKN automotive had four plants spread over the state of North Carolina, and the end product was half shafts for front wheel drive vehicles. If you climb under your front wheel drive car, you will see one part of the half shaft connects to your wheel (the outboard part) and the other to the transmission (the inboard part).

The first plant in the process was a large forging operation that made the housings for the inboard and outboard parts.

Product for forging went two directions; half to the inboard plant and half to the outboard plant. The inboard and outboard plants shipped to the assembly plant, where the shaft was put together and shipped. GKN had defined their system as a physical plant in a particular location. However, when we looked at the system, all of the equipment in the inboard and outboard plants was designated for a particular car type. The actual system that made sense was a particular value stream that correlated to a very specific auto type, such as a Toyota Camry. In each physical plant, they made half-shaft parts for twenty-two different vehicles; therefore we redefined the system as being twenty-two value lanes versus four physical plant locations. Although that may seem more complicated, it was actually a lot easier because workers began to identify with their value lane and end customer versus a plant location.

This simple move of redefining the system emphasized the interdependency required to service each specific customer auto line. All members of the value lane had access to the inventory of their parts in front of their specific assembly team and all had a common objective to service that specific assembly area. Although these workers were separated by physical location, they were pulled together by common purpose, such as insuring the Ford Taurus assembly line met their due-date-schedule.

Measures

Transformation and flow are where most measures reside. I have heard many a management guru say, "Show me how you measure me, and I will show you how I behave. If you measure me in a stupid manner, do not complain if I do stupid things."

There are two reasons for measures:

1. External reporting

2. Internal control

External reporting is what we must do for outsiders–the government and the investment community. In the U.S., those translate to adhering to Generally Accepted Accounting Principles, GAAP. We have found that those are terrible measures for one to use to improve internal control. Unfortunately, many still apply the principles of GAAP to operations.

I think the farther away from global measures one gets, the more dangerous those measures become because they may not align with the overall goal. For internal control we want a measurement system that measures the impact of a local action on the overall goal of the organization. Let me give an example.

When I was at Sherwin-Williams, I had four operating units that reported to me. One of those units was a plant that made highway paint. Highway paint is the white and yellow lines we are all supposed to notice while driving down the road. In that plant, I had eight thousand-gallon tanks, which is a big tank in the industry. I also made only two colors, and the plant was laid out very efficiently. All of this meant that I had very low cost relative to everyone else in the company. In addition to highway paint, I also produced a low-end paint that is used in factories called *dry fall*. The product gets its name because when sprayed it will dry before it hits the ground so it will not mess up equipment and can be swept up. The sales folks, who were compensated on margin, liked to sell their dry fall out of my plant because I had the lowest cost. My plant always had plenty of orders.

During the busy season I did not have the capacity to make all of the highway paint and the additional dry fall business. We had to make the highway paint because it was contract business, so what was going to be left out was the dry fall business. That was fine with me (I wasn't in sales), so there was not a problem. However, our division president, who was a very smart man, made a new measure, and that was for every gallon in sales we lost in dry fall, because I could not produce it, he was going to charge my plant a dollar. I felt this was an unfair measure, but it did not matter what I thought. I now have a problem.

The solution to the problem was to offload my production to one of our other plants. I called my pal John Davidson, who ran the Garland, Texas facility. "John, I would like to offload my dry fall production to you for a couple of months." What I did not understand is that according to our bonus plan, John would take a negative variance by producing my product because of my very low standard cost for that particular paint. In his thick Texas drawl, he answered, "Boy, have you been smoking some of those funny cigarettes up there in Baltimore? There is no way that I am going to make that product." Now I do have a problem!

I called John again and asked him two questions:

1. If you take this business will you have to hire any additional people?

2. If you take this business will you have to invest in any more inventory?

The answer to both questions was no. "So, the only thing that will change if you do not take this order is that our competitor will. Correct?" Of course the answer to that question was yes, and John and I both had a good laugh about how stupid that would be. So we got our division controller on a conference call and got this worked out where he would not take a hit on negative variance to standard.

I think it is important to note that if our division president had not made that silly new rule that my plant would get charged for lost sales in dry fall, our competitor would have gotten a lot of new business at our expense. The local action we were trying to judge was, "Do we make dry fall paint in Garland, Texas, during the busy season?" In this case, the measurement system we had in place for external reporting did not properly guide our actions toward our goal to make money.

Each process that you employ to achieve your goal (sales, marketing, manufacturing, etc.) should have a key indicator of results in addition to the result measure. If you only measure the results, then you are looking in the rearview mirror. We need to measure behaviors that result in good performance. For example, in safety, if you measure only lost time accidents and recordable rates, then that is measuring by looking in the rear view mirror. We need to measure the behaviors that we know lead to good safety records.

Improvement Should be Easy

Gosh, there are only four things to fool with—dependency, capacity, variability, and inventory. In most manufacturing operations, dependency is pretty much set (although you should challenge it). People have made too much out of variability. Yes, it is important, but it does not have near the impact that capacity does. And inventory is simply stored capacity. So, what's the problem? This is incredibly simple. How come all organizations are not knocking the cover off the ball with respect to performance? Could it be those nasty old people?

Chapter 4

How Does the Leader Impact Flow?

This transformation and flow stuff is so simple; how do we mess it up? Transformation and flow would be easy if it were not embedded in those nasty old cultures. Those cultures where, "This is the way we have always done it," may be the unstated slogan of the day.

Let's take a look at Figure 2.

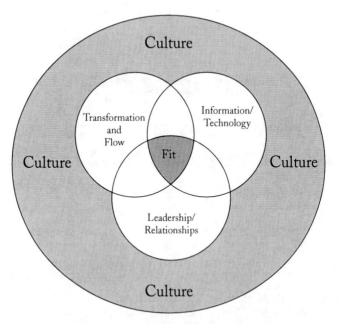

Figure 2. Enterprise Fitness Model

Steven Covey, the author of so many great leadership and self-improvement books, said that in order for an individual to improve they must improve in four areas: spiritual, physical, mental, and social. Steven Covey did not invent that thought process; I have heard the same thing from Pastor Sandy Taylor in one of her sermons. Pastor Taylor said that life is like a milk stool, and each one of the four legs stands for the four above-mentioned items. If one leg is neglected, then the stool tilts and is unbalanced. The stool could turn over.

Since organizations are made up of people, perhaps they are indeed like a milk stool also. As consultants, the folks at Chesapeake could never leave well enough alone, so we had to change what Pastor Taylor and Steven Covey said, and we incorporated it into transformation and flow, information, and leadership embedded in the culture that they form. I think one can use their imagination and see where the milk stool is still represented in all of that.

We have discussed transformation and flow (T&F). The "physical" is embedded in T&F. T&F is where measures and numbers lie. You go to the doctor get on the scale, get poked, pee in a cup, etc., and they come back with numbers relative to some measure of goodness or standard. My doctor always slants the numbers to make me appear fat. I think he is an unreasonable butthead. Depending upon their purpose, we find organizations measuring things like net profit, EBITDA, return on investment, due date performance, percent of members involved in missions, and starting salaries for new graduates. All of these measures address the success of your transformation and flow process.

For a moment, let's look at the relationship between culture and leadership. Do cultures create the leader or does the leader create the culture? That was a very important question for us at Chesapeake. We are lazy and do not want to have to focus on too many things. Both culture and leadership sound like pretty heavy subjects, so we would like to boil that down to one or the other.

I think we all can make a good argument for either scenario. When I left Sherwin-Williams, I was a much worse leader than when I walked into Sherwin-Williams. The S&W culture had a negative effect on me. Note how I am taking no personal responsibility for being a jerk and probably needing to be fired. We struggled with the issue. The following two questions helped us resolve it:

1. Can you mess up a great culture with a bad leader?

2. Can you fix a bad culture with a good leader?

We concluded that the answer to both questions was yes. Situation No. 2 is a tad more difficult, but it can be done. So, leaders are a cause and culture is an effect.

Imagine the picture of a farmer tending to an orchard. This agricultural image portrays this same scenario. The trees represent the transformation and flow process, and its effectiveness would be measured by the yield of fruit, moisture content of the fruit, etc. If the results were not what was wanted or expected, do we improve the situation by beating on the trees? One can spend a lot of effort beating on trees, but I would question the effectiveness of this action. Perhaps a better approach would be to analyze the soil (the culture) to see if it is missing something. Perhaps the soil needs more water or nutrients.

Who determines what action to take (or not take) with the soil? The farmer (the leadership) would be the one with that responsibility. Although I am sure this analogy makes sense to us, there are some hidden challenges. When the farmer puts something into the soil, there is not a loud bang and all of a sudden ripe apples start falling off the trees in record numbers. It may take time. There is somewhat of a leap of faith that what the farmer puts into the soil will work for the next harvest season. I think our organizations are the same. Somewhere along the line the leader needs to do the right thing, and that means they either know what to do themselves or trust others around them to know. They must also stay the course with a correct decision and not keep changing everything based on short-term noise.

After the Exodus of the Hebrew people from Egypt, a lot is learned by watching the relationship between God, his people, and the various leaders and kings. There seems to be a pattern—things are good, a bad leader lets things slip, things get bad, then a good leader gets things back on track. In 1 Kings 15:9–24 is the story of Asa, who was king of Judah, the southern kingdom of Israel. He took over from his father Abijah who really left behind a mess. Starting at verse eleven, "Asa did what was right in the eyes of the Lord, as his forefather David had done. He expelled the male shrine prostitutes from the land and got rid of all the idols his fathers had made. He even disposed of his grandmother Maacah from her position as queen mother, because she had made a repulsive Asherah pole." Asa ruled for forty-one years, and all was well. He was a good leader that went into a bad culture and turned it around.

The image of the farmer in the orchard brings us to Figure 3. I first saw this from a seminar put on by my good friend and leadership instructor Dr. John Grinnell. John claimed that those things above the line are management issues and those below the line are leadership issues. Most of us are in positions that require some of both skill sets. It is important to understand your role at any given time.

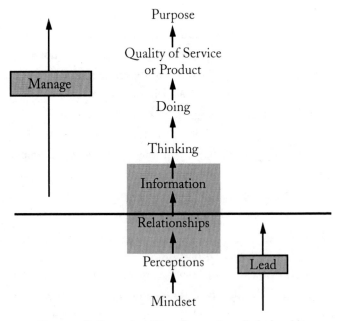

Figure 3. Information Flow Depends on Relationships

Pretend that you worked for a company that made large industrial engines and you are a sales rep. You start getting complaints from your customers that the engine is having quality problems, and it appears to be widespread. What do you do? Well, you are probably going to gather some information from the customer and take it back to the plant, where you and several others get together to exchange information and *think* about what is causing the problem and what should be done. After a good bit of head scratching, you and your work colleagues are going to *act* and *do* something. Assuming that what you came up with was a good idea and you executed it well, then the *quality* of the engines again meets the customer's expectations, and you achieve the *purpose* of a happy customer.

All of this just sounds great and is what you want to have happen. However, what if you think the chief engineer at the plant is an egotistical bozo? What if he thinks you are a pansy, overpaid sales rep? What if the team you put together to *think* about the issue does not trust one another? How well does the critical information flow? What if the implementation of the solution required several different departments to cooperate with one another and they were historical adversaries (research and operations). How hard would it be to achieve the goal under those conditions?

I worked for a paint company in Chattanooga, and I absolutely despised the two top sales people. I did not believe a word they told me, assuming their entire purpose in life was to try and make operations look bad to cover up their own ineptitude. I also assumed that they were the dumbest two people on the planet. Heck, they were sales guys! They couldn't be very smart or they would have a real job. Any doofus could sell paint. It took a real genius to make the paint.

I had a mindset that was probably not the best suited for an open and free flow of information. I would guess that they had a similar opinion of me and other folks in operations.

The fortunate thing about most of those mindsets (assumptions) is that they are wrong. Now that I have matured a tad, I am guessing that both of those gentlemen had some redeeming qualities and that if I had made half an effort that perhaps I could have exposed one or two of them. Imagine two people in a relationship and a pipe connecting their two heads. Let the pipe represent the relationship, and information flows through the pipe from one brain into the other. Now imagine crud building up in the pipeline that restricts the flow. That crud is like plaque in blood vessels. The crud represents erroneous assumptions that people have about one another and mistrust. Unless the crud is purged out, information flow is restricted or stopped all together.

So the reason one wants to improve relationships within an organization is not to have your people skipping through the tulips singing *Kum Ba Ya* but to better flow critical information. The tulip skipping might be a nice side effect, but it is not the reason you do it.

In dealing with even the toughest minded CEO, the logic in figure 3 rings true. I think it is an obvious way of connecting behavior and relationship issues with purpose and the core processes that cause purpose to happen.

Summary

Let's go back to figure 3 and focus on the bottom and the top of the diagram; mindset and purpose. Mindset is the attitude you, as the leader, bring concerning those you are connected to in the work environment. That mindset helps form your assumptions about those same folks. Purpose is the reason why your organization exists and includes the specific processes that achieve purpose. If we concentrate on those two things, we are going to be way ahead of the game on becoming better leaders and creating a culture that is conducive to improvement.

So how does the leader impact flow? The leader is the one responsible for the culture, and the flow system resides in the culture. The better the culture, the more it inspires good flow of ideas and work.

Chapter 5
The Leadership Model

Our Search for a Model

Okay, so our gang decided that we needed to come up with a leadership development offering. In many cases, in order to succeed with a client, our consultants had to supply a disproportionate part of the leadership that the client should be providing. That fact increased the amount of time we were at the clients' facility, and thus we were unable to accept new jobs. Our consultants are excellent, and I can see why our customers wanted them to assume more. All of our folks have frontline leadership experience. I like to tell people that we only hire people who have been in a position where if they made a stupid decision, something bad would happen quickly, and they lived with the consequences. Frontline leaders seem to understand that.

In bad situations, either the client leaned on us too much to provide leadership and thus were at risk of going backwards once we left, or they were so dysfunctional that we essentially took over for awhile. Neither of those situations is good.

What we set out to develop was new for us. We had a lot of experience delivering process improvement expertise, but how do we teach *leadership?* Many of us had been through leadership learning experiences at service academies, work, etc. As a company, we agreed to launch a journey to learn. Lord knows there are a bazillion folks out there that claim to teach leadership.

We found two models of leadership; one we will call an attribute model and the other a self-awareness model.

At one of our company meetings, we paid to have a PhD and his wife, also a PhD, teach us their version of leadership development, which was the attribute model. I forget how many attributes they had, but it was a boatload. They would test us as individuals and as a group and then do sort of a gap analysis where they pointed out our biggest weaknesses. The plan was then for us to improve on those attributes so we could become like their model leader. With their model, you would spend the rest of your life trying to be someone else. It was a massive waste of money and did not work for us.

Not long after the bad attribute experience, I was on a plane and struck up a conversation with the fellow next to me. We eventually got around to what each other did, and he said that his company worked on leadership development. I told him that he had a potential sale with me. This fellow worked for Dr. Jim Farr who had his own institute. Their model was based on self-awareness where a leader becomes aware of how their style affects others and thus can adapt when appropriate. This seemed to make a bit more sense.

At this particular time, it was our intention to partner with an organization for our leadership product/service. So, in addition to looking for a model that we were comfortable with, we were also looking for a partner that shared our values.

I agreed to go to one of their sessions, and at one point, I found myself lying on the floor in a dark room, listening to the sound track of the *Last of the Mohicans's*, while many of the people lying around me were wailing about how they had been abused by their parents. I was trying to imagine one of our corporate clients going through this experience and was coming up blank. I was also looking for the emergency exit.

We did not find anyone we felt comfortable with. Most of the people we ran into held a PhD, did not have any leadership experience, and felt that they had invented air and water. A lack of humility seemed to be a common thread for many of these leadership gurus. There were some notable exceptions, one being my friend Dr. John Grinnell, whom I mentioned earlier.

We then went off on a journey to hire some leadership development talent. That worked a little better, but again, we got mostly people who had not sat in the chair. I have always had a bias in favor of people who had actually been leaders. Our experience with hiring people who claimed to be leadership experts was also somewhat of a failure, although we did make progress on developing our own model.

The Enterprise Leadership Model

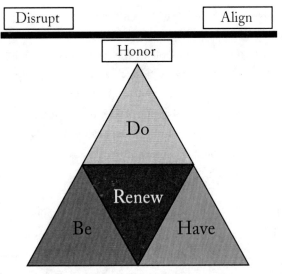

Figure 4 The Enterprise Leadership Model

Figure 4 is our Enterprise Leadership Model, and the essential roles and aspects are depicted by triangles. At the very top of the model, we see the specific actions of leadership. We see three roles that are ongoing for a leader:

1. Disrupt

2. Align

3. Honor

We will get back to the details of each of those roles in a little while. Let's complete the model first.

The *Have* portion of the model is where concepts and assumptions lie. It is how the leader sees things. When we see something in reality, we check that against some concept we already have and then make a judgment. My wonderful wife, Linda, gave me a poster for my office, which reads, "FAITH: seeing is not believing; believing is seeing." I am sort of dense, so I stared at that thing for years and didn't get it. Finally it dawned on me that we only see something if we first believe it exists.

In learning something new, like Lean, Six Sigma, or the Theory of Constraints, it is the *Have* portion of the model that is changed. Someone already has a perception of how their plant or business should operate, and that is based on their experiences. When we help a client, we must be successful in changing their perception, or else the implementation and improvement will not be long lasting. That is why we see so much value in hands-on educational tools.

The *Be* portion of the model may be where character resides. Words like authentic, trustworthy, courageous, consistent, and persistent come to mind. It may also be where emotional intelligence exists.

Renew is almost self-explanatory. Even God rested on the seventh day, so any model of improvement needs some sort of rejuvenation. Cows do not stay milked. It just stands to reason that in order to be the best that we can be, we must constantly renew ourselves by proper exercise/diet, spiritual development, being with friends and family in a social setting, and stretching our minds by learning and thinking.

The *Have, Be, and Renew* are the base that supports the *Do* (action) of our model.

Chapter 6

Have

The *Have* part of our pyramid is what you know, believe, and assume to be true. It contains your assumptions about life and has been influenced by your life's journey. Included is your education, work experience, and just about anything that you have experienced during your waking hours on earth.

"Actions can only be understood within the contexts, or frameworks. Great leaders look at ideas, plans, and decisions within a number of different contexts. This is the adaptability that might lead one to say, for example, that a particular course of action could be profitable in the short-term but disastrous over the long haul. Understanding essential organizational perspectives informs and orients leaders, and helps them make good decisions." (*Taken from page 16 of Chesapeake Consulting Leadership Strengths Profile*)

I think the *Have* is almost like those super computers that play chess. You put in some initial rules, and as the computer gets trounced by masters of the game it learns and retains what it learns. As time goes on, the computer gets a lot better as its list of valid things to compare becomes more robust. Soon the computer is almost impossible to beat.

Any consultant in process improvement normally is dealing with the gap in the *Have* between what they know and what their client knows. That knowledge may be how to flow material through a system or how to get a new flow system implemented.

We started our business on the principles of the Theory of Constraints (TOC). People that would call us were those that were having a business problem that they felt TOC would address. TOC is a different way of looking at an organization, and for us to be successful, we needed to first spend a lot of time transferring knowledge to the *Have* portion of our clients. That process involved classroom training, late night discussions where we would draw on napkins and move silverware and salt and peppershakers around to illustrate our points.

In part of the classroom training, we use hands on simulations and computer simulations that are business models. The goal of each simulation is to get the most money and/or product out of the system. The vast, vast majority of people fail miserably in their first attempt. Of course, that is what we expect. They are trying to solve the problem of not enough throughputs by using the contents in their *Have.* Their *Have* does not include constraint management and in fact probably contains information that is opposite. A lot of learning takes place when they fail with their existing *Have* but succeed with their newfound knowledge, which begins to alter their *Have*. Pretty cool. It is an ongoing process and really gets cemented when the customer actually uses the concepts in their real business and gets results.

Every person and organization starts at a different place. For example, some folks already have a head start on TOC with respect to their knowledge base. In the early 1990s, one of our consultants Matti Hertzberg and I were giving one of our two-day workshops at the Rohm & Haas facility in Bristol. As we walked in the gate, I told Matti, "These people will do better than anyone we have ever had run the simulators." Matti disagreed and mumbled something in Hebrew so I wouldn't understand what he said. I had a little inside information and knew that most of the people in the class were chemical engineers and during their education had to do material and energy balances where they had to find the "bottleneck." Mattie was amazed that about half the class maxed out the simulator on the first try. Aside from that group, I can count the number of people that have maxed it on the first try without having to take off my shoes and use my toes to count. And that is in twenty years of doing it. The people at Rohm & Haas already had that concept as part of their internal framework because they were accustomed to looking for bottlenecks.

It is important to note that since all people and organizations start with a different *Have,* exactly the same approach does not work for everyone. A skilled teacher or consultant must be able to determine where an organization is today so they can help them map a course for tomorrow. It has been my experience that this takes some experience.

Have is Where Unifying Purpose Resides

Several times I will take us back to our basic principle that organizations are held together by *purpose, relationships,* and *information.* In the *Have* portion of our model, there must reside a clear and unifying purpose. The degree to which relationships are built is a huge factor in determining the rate and quality of information flow.

It is interesting that often people in organizations are confused or ignorant about that essential focusing element—purpose. Either they have lost touch with the purpose over time, or circumstances, such as market changes, have rendered a previous purpose obsolete. Absent a clear purpose, focus is nearly impossible. There are a variety of ways to come up with unifying purpose. When working with clients, we have found it to be an engaging and messy process from the standpoint that there is not one cookie cutter approach. Any process that causes some good discernment will work.

Jim Collins in his book *Good to Great* does a good job in getting folks to ask:

- What are we passionate about?
- What can we be the best in the world at?
- What is our economic engine?

He calls the alignment of the answers to these questions to be the "Hedgehog" concept.

John Covington

Another book we have used in working with clients is *The Discipline of Market Leaders* by Treacy and Wiersema. I think both these books help a company go through the struggle that is necessary to evolve purpose and identity.

As we mentioned in the transformation and flow chapter, an understanding of the process by which purpose is achieved is fundamental knowledge and needs to reside in the *Have* of our leaders so they can communicate it and have it reside in the *Have* of their followers. It has been my experience that this is lacking in most organizations. Many people have purpose down pat but when asked, "Explain to me how you go about 'fixing ships' or 'making Disciples' or 'making money,'" they lose their clarity of thinking. Having that clarity is a huge advantage in improving overall performance.

Long Term View

When purpose is clear and well established in your *Have*, it is easier to make long-term decisions. When purpose is unclear and immediate shareholder value is the mainstay, then short-term results dominate.

We have observed some leaders sacrifice long-term good for short-term gain. I think the most obvious example of this is someone shipping marginally good product that is at risk of being returned. The company will be able to invoice it this month and get all of the short-term gains of doing so. But what happens if the customers are dissatisfied with the quality of service and product? What will be the long-term effect?

If there is not clarity with regard to purpose, then many decisions are not as clear-cut and can be rationalized. This may cause people to get caught up into firefighting mode and not pay attention to decisions that will take them closer to their purpose in the long term. This, of course, causes more fires to fight. This has been a leadership issue since the beginning of time. My friend and client Jeff Bust says that it is like running a race with no end.

Of the three basic foundations of our model, *Be, Have,* and *Renew,* the one you can effect most in the short-run is *Have.* As a leader, you want to make sure that you do an excellent job of communicating purpose to your team to the point where it becomes a fixture within their *Have.*

Chapter 7

Be

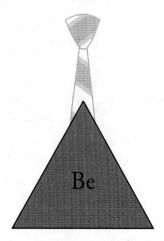

Whereas *Have* is mastering context, *Be* is mastering self. A variety of words roll off our tongues when we think about *Be*—authentic, courageous, consistent, honest, ethical, and emotionally intelligent. *Be* can also be thought of as temperament, which is an emotional thing rather than logic.

Have you ever had a boss that when they walked into the room they just sucked the energy out of the place? Have you ever had a boss that stole from you or intentionally changed data to foster their point of view? Do you have experience with a leader who is obsessed with company politics? Do you know a few people that are just general buttheads? If so, then you have a feel for someone who is lacking some *Be*.

Be in the leadership model consists of a set of traits or *character* and has a profound impact on personal destiny. It is more powerful in determining success than IQ or anything that might be in the *Have* triangle. In fact, the quality of the *Be* triangle will be reflected in the quality of the *Have, Do,* and *Renew,* although they are so interdependent that they flow into one another multiple ways.

None of us is perfect in our *Be* part of leadership, but let's just go over some extremes so we can get the point.

We were working with a textile company in North Carolina that had opened a sales office in New York City. The company sent one of their good ole boys up to manage the new sales office and customer relations. During one sales meeting with several apparel customers, one of the customers jumped up on the conference room table and began ranting about poor quality and a litany of other issues. During the process, the customer kicked some fabric, and it landed on the new head of sales. Bubba promptly stood up, snatched the poor customer by the collar, and cold cocked him. I think by the time the customer regained consciousness, Bubba had been recalled to the Tar Heel state.

I had a boss who was delinquent in turning my bonus plan into personnel. He was supposed to have gotten the package to me and have me signoff on it by a certain date. What he did, was never send it to me and traced my name from another document I had signed. This is the same boss that when a government helicopter flew over our site to check on some environmental issues he flipped them the international sign of ill will. I told him, "Dave, I certainly hope they do not have a camera onboard and that your picture does not makes the front page of the *Baltimore Sun.*"

I had another boss, Mr. Ned Kemlein, who was a wonderful role model. Ned was president of a small paint company in Atlanta, and I was the director of manufacturing. What I remember about Ned was the way he handled himself, not so much by what he did. However, what he did must have been good because we ran twice the profit percentage of the industry average. Two incidents with Ned stuck with me. One time we were walking to a meeting when a salesman happened to drop in to see me without an appointment. The salesman approached me in the lobby as we were walking to Mr. Kemlein's office. I was short-tempered with the man and let him know that I was currently busy and I could not see him. When we got behind closed doors, Mr. Kemlein said to me, "John, you were rude to that man." Talk about catching me off balance. He was correct, and he really taught me a lesson by calling me on it. I probably am still rude on occasion, but that quick lecture has saved me from many additional incidents where I might make someone feel small versus make them feel important and respected.

After our company was sold, Mr. Kemlein was going to retire. He pulled me aside and told me that he had underestimated my ability and potential and that he should have picked me as the new president of the company, despite my young age. He did not have to say that, but it sure made a young whippersnapper feel mighty good.

Mr. Kemlein was also totally intolerant of immoral behavior and set a wonderful example for his staff and employees.

There was just a sense that Mr. Kemlein would always do the right thing and not be swayed by personal gain.

What is good temperament versus bad temperament? I don't know, but I think I recognize it when I see it. I also think you can test for it to an extent. Also, if a person is serious about improving their *Be,* then I think they can. If *Be* is not in some sort of decent order, then the chances of being a good leader are not good.

One trait that is a reflection of good *Be* is humility. Imagine a test tube filled with water and oil. Imagine the water as God or purpose centered and the oil as self-centered. All of us possess both oil and water in our personal test tubes; it is just a matter of degree. The more water the better. Humility is akin to that servant leadership thing we hear about.

Warren was the best pastor I recall. First of all, he was successful. Under his leadership, the church he led grew to the point where you could not get another car in the parking lot. There were numerous new Bible studies and mission projects. There was collaboration with an African-American Church in the community, which fostered better understanding and good will. He was forced to retire at seventy, and after fifteen years of his absence, the church is just a fraction of what it was. People did not stop going to church, they just stopped going to that Methodist church. What I remember about Warren was that he was loving and humble. I do not think I ever heard him utter an unkind word about anyone.

I am going to estimate that our church is about one-third the size and vitality that it was when Warren left. There were three pastors that followed him. None of the three had the characteristics of humble servant leader; rather, they felt a need to control. Each was a bully in his own way. I think this may be the opposite of humble. The result of these three leaders was devastating for this church.

Romans 12:3–5 addresses the issues of humility and honoring, "For by the grace given me I say to every one of you: Do not think of yourself more highly than you ought, but rather think of yourself with sober judgment, in accordance with the measure of faith God has given you. Just as each of us has one body with many members, and these members do not all have the same function, so in Christ we who are many form one body, and each member belongs to all the others."

The *Be* part of our model is the most difficult to write about because there is so much judgment involved. None of us are perfect, so it is uneasy discussing issues of character that reside in *Be*. Some of the hard questions to ask might be:

- Can people believe what you tell them?
- Can your employees, bosses, and peers trust that you will not say or imply bad things about them?
- Do you put your team above personal gain?
- Can people rely on you?
- Do you appreciate the work of others?
- Do you create an environment where people around you are made to feel at ease and not threatened?
- When things go bad do you take the blame, and when things go good do you give credit elsewhere?
- Do you show the courage to address poor performance and bad behavior with those that are responsible?
- Are you setting a good example?

Christ tells us that we can determine a tree by the fruit that it bears. Again we can look to Paul to throw some wisdom out concerning good fruit in Galatians 5:22–23b, "But the fruit of the Spirit is love, joy, peace, patience, kindness, goodness, and self-control." When I reflect back, that describes Mr. Kemlein and Pastor Warren, who were both successful leaders.

We all fall short on some of these items—I know I do. One of the most revered leaders in all of history is King David. If you have ever flown El Al, you know that they call their first class section the King David section. However, even King David had his warts. He had an affair with the wife of one of his troops and eventually had the man murdered to cover up the affair. And we thought Bill Clinton acted poorly. The point is that even the best leaders mess up and do bad and stupid things.

Improving our batting average on doing good things will serve to improve our *Be* and help us develop into better leaders. Many people improve their *Be* after some sort of significant emotional event, such as a heart attack. I have used Rohm & Haas as a good example several times and made reference to their culture. Remember, leaders are responsible for the culture, and I must give a lot of credit to my old pal Frank Trotta, who I mentioned earlier. He was the vice president of global operations and was the fellow in charge during all of those good changes. Frank was a fun fellow to be around and had a funny abrasive edge to him. He acted a lot tougher than he was.

I recall talking with some of the other R&H managers that worked for Frank, all of which were a lot younger than him. We all began to realize that most took Frank for granted. However, if you stopped and looked at all that was accomplished under his leadership, it was significant. Then, one of the fellows spoke up and said, "You know, Frank was not always like that. At one time he was one hundred pounds overweight, had a terrible temper, and people just did not like being around him. He had a terrible reputation." Somewhere along the line Frank made a choice to improve his *Be,* and obviously it worked. Not only was Frank an effective leader, but he was also in decent shape, having lost a lot of weight. Several years after we completed our initial work with Rohm & Haas, Frank died of cancer. Frank is another leader I would like to lift up as one that made a difference in people's lives. Many of those that he mentored are making a contribution at Rohm & Haas today.

I am not suggesting that you go out and eat a boxcar load of pork rinds to induce a heart attack just so you can improve your *Be*. There is bound to be a better way for us to put things in perspective and place important issues like our health and relationships first. Perhaps we can "pretend" something really scary happens to us and ask ourselves how we would act differently if we had another chance.

Chapter 8

Renew

Dr. Mike Umble is a neat friend that I met through the TOC community. Mike is a management professor at Baylor University, and at one time we were trying to write a book together. During our time together in Waco, Texas, Mike used the phrase, "Cows don't stay milked." I laughed then, and I still laugh because it is so true. You cannot exercise one week and be done with it—darn!

Actually writing this book is a form of renewal for me. Instead of giving up something for Lent this year, I decided to add something. By the way, that is the same way as giving up something because we only have twenty-four hours a day, and I am not going to give up any more sleep. During Lent I promised I would write every day and replace working crosswords with exercise.

Many times *Renew* gets put on the back burner because it does not appear urgent. It is important to understand that rarely is the urgent neither important nor the important urgent. We all get sucked into the urgency of the day, and it takes discipline to do those exercises, take that time for spiritual reading, prayer, and discernment.

Why Renew?

Tiger Woods may evolve as the greatest golfer to ever play the game. What is the difference between Sam Snead, Arnold Palmer, Jack Nicholas, and Tiger Woods? In my opinion, Tiger is in much better physical shape than any of the aforementioned golfers. The others were natural athletes, but did they dedicate the time and effort to the physical conditioning that Tiger does? I think that is the difference maker.

I'm sure when you are doing sit-ups, push-ups, running, weight lifting, and pull-ups that it is hard to relate that effort to shooting a 62 at Pebble Beach. However, Tiger has the discipline to do this because he takes a leap of faith that doing the right things causes things to go right. There is no instant gratification in renewal activities.

Renewal is also counterintuitive. John Wesley, the founder of the Methodist Movement, once said that he had so much to do that he needed to pray more. That makes no sense. If you need more time to get your work done, why would you spend extra time doing renewal? Because it is the smart thing to do. I do not know of anyone who got as much accomplished in their lifetime as John Wesley, and he did it by adhering to simple rules of nature, which include exercise, eating properly, spiritual development, and his job created mental and social opportunities.

I work with a lot of CEOs and vice presidents of companies. These have always been high-pressure jobs, but I believe today we are making them more high pressure than they need to be. I see an increasing number of executives spend little or no time with family. They are on planes to Asia, in hotels throughout the U.S. and foreign countries, and in apartments because they did not move their family to their new job location. I am going to give some somber examples then move on.

Several years ago we did business with a one hundred-million-dollar generic pharmaceutical company. It was a very high-pressure environment, and it seems like they were always in some sort of crisis mode. Long hours, long meetings, constant cell phones ringing, and weekend work. They accomplished their business goals, were eventually purchased (one of the goals), and several folks made a lot of money and were off to their next assignment. There were five top executives including the CEO. Within two years after the purchase there were two deaths (one specifically stress related) and one divorce. Having all that business success meant nothing to at least sixty percent of the executive team.

You have heard this before, but it is worth repeating—I do not know of anyone who on their deathbed wished they had spent more time at work. Also, the planet and probably your company will get along just fine without all your toil.

The key to productivity is the beauty of the "AND." How can you be very productive AND spend time being with loved ones and doing those things required for renewal.

How to Renew

Renewal activities give you capacity to do more work and to absorb those periods of time where your capacity and resources are stretched.

There are four areas of renewal:

1. Spiritual

2. Social

3. Physical

4. Mental

They are all important, and if you neglect one of the four you will be out of balance.

Let me see if we can come up with some helpful hints for each category. On *Spiritual*, I am going to yield to my old buddy John Wesley again. I am going to make the assumption that you believe in God. John Wesley talked about being on the path to spiritual formation, and he said there were seven areas:

1. Worship joyously. This means getting together with several other folks on a routine basis and worshiping God.

2. Pray and study daily. Spend time alone with your God and yourself. Ponder your holy book and discern life choices.

3. Participate in the Sacraments

4. Fast. This does not necessarily mean a food fast, but that is the most common type.

5. Talk with others about how God is working in your life and share your story.

6. Participate in acts of mercy.

7. Address injustice.

Again, this is very "Methodist," but this general plan should work regardless of your beliefs.

Social is an opportunity to get away from those that are in your work environment. I have a dear friend who is a bishop. In his denomination, that is as high as you go. One of my nuggets of advice to him is to find some people to hang with where he isn't bishop, he is just John. That could be college classmates, friends in the neighborhood, relatives, parents of your children's friends, or some sort of special interest like bike riding or hunting.

What I do for *Mental* is work crossword puzzles and Sudoku games. I may have carried this one to an extreme, and if I do not gear this down a tad my lovely wife, Linda, is going to shoot me. We get four newspapers per day, and each one has a crossword puzzle and a Sudoku game. They can become addictive, so be careful.

I am not going to say *Physical* is more important, but it can be the hardest to maintain. Some of the simple stuff—

get physicals when you are supposed to and try to eat sensibly. Drink water, because dehydration is one of the largest sappers of energy. Get outside and get some exercise daily, especially if your job calls for you to be inside.

The *Renew* portion of our pyramid determines how much energy you bring to your leadership role. Your energy will spark more energy in your organization because your folks can feel it.

The Apostle Paul links physical and mental renewal to good decision making. In Romans 12:1–2 he writes, "Therefore, I urge you, brothers, in view of God's mercy, to offer your bodies as living sacrifices, holy and pleasing to God—which is your spiritual worship. Do not conform any longer to the pattern of this world, but be transformed by the renewing of your mind. Then you will be able to test and approve what God's will is–his good, pleasing, and perfect will."

It is critically important so get that calendar out and schedule your renewal activities.

Chapter 9

Do

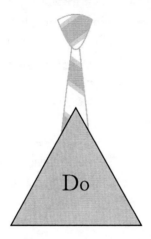

Now that we have the foundations of *Be, Have,* and *Renew,* let's address leadership action. What do leaders *Do?* Before we start, it is again important to stress that most people in a leadership position have management tasks as well as leadership responsibilities. Part of being effective is knowing when to put on what hat.

In our Enterprise Fitness Leadership Model, we portray the essential aspects of leadership; who is the leader (*Be*), what do they know and believe (*Have*); how much energy do they bring to the table (*Renew*), and how do they act (*Do*).

There are three roles of a leader that we should see: Disrupting, Aligning, and Honoring.

I think perhaps the biggest difference in leading and managing is that in order to lead, one must disrupt. Even to maintain the status quo, one must disrupt behavior that tends to stray away from the norm. Everything is always in motion, and if you want any say in where the motion is going, you had best be ready to disrupt. Being disruptive is not natural for some folks, and we will need some techniques to make it easier.

Disrupting, Honoring, and *Aligning* are all done simultaneously. Before you start disrupting the status quo, you should have some level of confidence that the next state of affairs is going to be better. Either you personally have an idea of where things will begin to settle, or you have faith in the people you are collaborating with that they will take you to that place. All of these actions must be done by honoring those people and principles you are connected to and accountable for.

Organizational Systems are Not Led, They are Disrupted.

I think the best way of describing *Disrupt, Honor,* and *Align* is through a series of examples.

When I headed manufacturing operations, I always inherited ones that were not doing so hot. The first thing I would do is put in the DuPont STOP system, which is a safety program based on changing attitudes. There was a method to my madness. Safety performance is something that can be measured, and if a facility is not doing well in one aspect of performance there is a good chance that all aspects are suffering, including safety. Putting in a successful safety program is something I knew how to do, and I had 100 percent confidence that it would work and yield results. I knew that I could take the team through a disruptive change that had a very specific goal and that they would win and achieve that goal. If they won at anything under my leadership, then someone would actually begin to think that this new fellow was someone they might want to listen to. Every facility I managed had well over one million man-hours without a lost time accident, and at one time, that was pretty good.

The program focused on supervisors observing unsafe acts, unsafe conditions, and then taking corrective action and steps to prevent recurrence. STOP had eight weekly training sessions and between the sessions the supervisors were supposed to take action by filling out an observation card. The managers would nod their head during the class and look really interested, but they had no intention of actually doing anything. After all, this is just another hair-brained session by the most current hair-brained plant manager. The first shock came on the next Monday morning when my secretary contacted each of them that had not turned in their cards. "Whoa, you mean you actually wanted us to do that?" They learned that even if they cheated, they needed to turn in those cards. It was a huge disruption. Soon we required hardhats and safety glasses. The aisles and floors were expected to be cleared of tripping hazards and gunk. Lock-out tags were required, and soon an entire new culture began to emerge based on that initial disruption.

One of the things the program taught is how to respond to people reacting to your presence. For example, if I walked into the plant and saw someone scrambling to put on his safety glasses and we made eye contact, then that was a critical moment. If I were to ignore this, then I sent a message. What I would *do* was immediately speak to the individual and explain why we wore safety glasses. This in itself is a disruptive act. To stop and walk over to that person's workstation versus continue going where I was headed is disruptive. Also, the contact was done with concern and honor, with the idea that the person made an honest error in failing to wear their protective equipment.

Asking questions is disruptive behavior for a leader. "What are you doing? What would happen if we moved that machine over to building three? What do we need to do to get more production?" If you are the boss, just hanging around a particular work area might be disruptive.

Honoring

Let's face it. There are some folks in your work place you like being around, and there are some folks you do not like. Any dope can get along with the folks they like. An effective leader learns to like everyone, even those that are unlikable and/or different.

One of my favorite parts of the Bible is 1 Corinthians chapters 12 and 13. Chapter 12 starts by talking about individuals being different and having specific talents. It goes on to discuss how they all come together to make a whole and that each is important. One of the things this chapter emphasizes is that no one part is more important than the others. Dr. Gary April was one of my college professors and is now a great friend. One of the things he tries to convey to new college graduates is that they are no more important than anyone else in the organization. He tells them that they were given special abilities and thus have a responsibility to use those abilities for the common good. He is a wise friend and always the professor.

Visualize a high school chemistry model of a molecule with the different sized balls connected by different sized sticks. Let the balls represent people and the sticks represent the relationships between those people. Chapter 12 discusses the individuals and Chapter 13 discusses the nature of the relationship. Many of us at our weddings had Chapter 13 read because it is the one on love. I have included these chapters in the appendix. If you have a moment, read them from the perspective of different individuals amassed for a particular goal and how they should relate to one another.

Honoring is actually loving your employees, peers, and superiors for who they are. Each one of them is a child of God and is deserving of your love. Some of them may not behave worth a flip, but that is another issue.

I have found and I have counseled others that when you decide not to respect and love anyone that reports to you, then it is time for one of you to hit the road. Honoring is very active and requires discernment and outright prayer.

When I have a major problem with relationships at work, I pray that I will be a better boss, I pray for the relationship between God and me, between the individual and God, and between me and the individual. Does that work? I think so. Sometimes, what we discover is that it is time to say our goodbyes. That is not necessarily a bad thing. Perhaps you were meant to be together for a period of time and that time is over.

The way you feel about someone will be absorbed by that person, and that is how they will probably act. If you feel someone is weak and sorry, that is what you will see and project. If you think they are great, they may perform great. You are the one who controls what you think, and that is honoring. Once you get to the point with someone where you cannot do that, then it's over. Let me again reference the poster Linda gave me: "FAITH: Seeing is not believing; Believing is seeing." You must believe something before you can see it. You must believe in the excellence and potential of your folks before you see it. If over time you try that and it doesn't work, you can always fire their sorry fanny. However, you may want to give that faith thing a chance.

Those last five paragraphs may be the most radical in the book because relationships are taken to a different level than normal in a business or organizational environment. I would encourage you to go to that level. However if love is too tough a word for you to ponder in the work environment, try respect. It is not quite as deep, but it gets you in the area. If you are not given to praying for those in your sphere of influence, you will still want to consider what you are going to do different to enhance a relationship. Whatever you do, it will require focus, thinking, and planning. The mere fact that a relationship has come to the forefront may mean there are problems. I have not run into many bad people. I have run into some bad misunderstandings and people that may be in the wrong job.

If misunderstanding is the issue, try this simple tactic. Given a particular topic of concern, write down what you think about the issue and what you think the other party thinks. Then get them to do the same thing. More than likely you will have surfaced an erroneous assumption which will purge out some of that crud we talked about, thus you will have improved the relationship. The main point is that you as the leader must take time to focus on the relationship or it will not improve.

Sometimes it may be necessary to get a little tough, especially if you are taking over a facility that is a poor performer. I took over a Sherwin-Williams facility that was an absolute mess. After I had been there a couple of months, my maintenance engineer challenged me at a staff meeting, "Why should we do anything that you say? Plant managers come and go, and you will not be here all that long." I pondered my response. "Well, Walt, one reason is that if you do not do what I say, then you will not be here to see me leave." And he wasn't.

We must also honor the organization. In the case of Walt, I must honor Walt for who he is, however, he was a poor performer and had a negative impact on our plant culture. If I had not fired Walt, I would have dishonored the organization and those employees that were trying to make the plant a better place to work. There came a point in the relationship with Walt where it was over. It is a mindset issue that what we see depends on what we are thinking before we look. There comes a point to where readjusting our thinking becomes too difficult, and we have to act based upon where our thoughts are at that time.

There will always be some folks with whom you have dealt where it is over because you have made the decision to not trust them to do a good job (remember—trust is always a decision on your part). Part of honoring is making the tough decision to say goodbye.

Alignment

I have heard Steven Covey say that you should begin with the end in mind. Either that or some variation of that is essential for alignment. What does the end resemble? What are some of the necessary elements? If you can determine that, then you can drive to the point where you and your team know the things to do to place them there.

Alignment to purpose, thus clarity about the processes that yield that purpose, is absolutely essential. I personally think that is the problem with mainstream religion. They are not past the tipping point on understanding what they make and what the process looks like. By not having this nailed down, individuals are left to come up with their own purpose, and now you have a mess on your hands.

Sometimes when you are crystal clear on purpose, some may opt out. That is okay. The clear purpose may not be in the direction they want to go.

The NASA janitor knew why he was coming to work and how his tasks were going to help put a man on the moon. Lack of clarity along the lines of alignment to purpose is one of the most common problems I see. Lack of clarity translates to lack of effective communications by the leadership team. Many leaders communicate something and then they think everyone understands it. I fall into that trap. Over communicating purpose is one of the main ways to achieve alignment.

We were doing some work for the general board of discipleship of the Methodist Church. We had asked them to draw a picture of their system and what they do. They are a very creative group and came back with some works of art—flowing rivers, models, pictures, and each had a poetic description of what they did. We sat there awed at their talent, but they didn't have anything with which we could work. One of our consultants got up and led them through the development of a process flow diagram. It was tedious. In the end, all were scratching their chin and pondering the diagram. One fellow spoke up and said, "You know, I like our art better. However, I actually understand the process diagram." The process flow diagram showed the specific actions or operations in the order in which they must occur to create the results that achieves their purpose. It helps bring clarity to what they were trying to accomplish.

Sometimes, especially in larger institutions, the institution becomes the purpose rather than the purpose for which the institution was formed. This problem can be avoided and/or corrected by being familiar with the processes that achieve your purpose and then seeing if that is where you have deployed resources.

For alignment, we need to have clarity of both purpose and the process by which it is achieved. Then our management activity is centered around monitoring those few things that gauge how well our purpose is being achieved and taking those actions that constantly nudge our process into better alignment.

Combining Disrupt, Honor, and Align

One of the reasons I went to work for Sherwin-Williams was Frank Butler. Frank was president of our consumer division. I had originally hired on to manage the S&W facility in Morrow, Georgia, and was in Cleveland for my last set of interviews. I already had the job offer when Frank wanted to have a private lunch with me. He explained that although he knew I had signed on for Morrow, he had a major problem in Baltimore and would I mind going there for two to three years. Frank was smart, successful, easy going, and put everyone around him at ease. Of course I would go to Baltimore.

After I had been there awhile, Frank came down for a visit, and he wanted to just spend some time with me in the conference room drinking coffee and shooting the bull. He said, "John, what would it look like if we were to start all over again here? If we were to get out a blank piece of paper, what would we need to run a paint facility?" I was too naïve to realize what he was doing (zero-based budgeting) so I took the bait hook, line, and sinker. We talked for hours down to every detail—how many security guards it would take, accounting, etc. Frank had been taking notes the whole time. When we were done, Frank had this big smile on his face and handed me a piece of paper. "John, here is what you said it would take to run the facility and here is how many folks you have now. We need to get your head count in line." Gulp!

The disruption part of this was obvious—that piece of paper with my new head count requirement. All during the discussion he was aligning as we painted a picture of what a new facility would look like and who would be doing what. It was sort of exciting and not just a head count reduction exercise. I always felt honored around Frank because he made you feel like a million dollars and that your opinion was the most important one in the world. Although he never studied the Chesapeake Leadership Model, he did pretty darn good.

John Covington

Chapter 10
Improvement Process

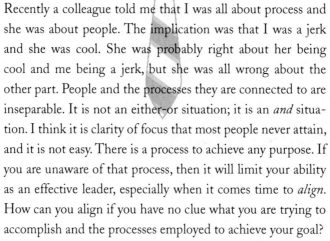

Recently a colleague told me that I was all about process and she was about people. The implication was that I was a jerk and she was cool. She was probably right about her being cool and me being a jerk, but she was all wrong about the other part. People and the processes they are connected to are inseparable. It is not an either-or situation; it is an *and* situation. I think it is clarity of focus that most people never attain, and it is not easy. There is a process to achieve any purpose. If you are unaware of that process, then it will limit your ability as an effective leader, especially when it comes time to *align*. How can you align if you have no clue what you are trying to accomplish and the processes employed to achieve your goal?

In order to start a fire we must have fuel, oxygen, and a source of ignition. Take away one of the three and the fire goes away. That is what we are saying about organizational systems; we must have *purpose* and *relationships*. Again, I am making the assumption that information is held by individuals making use of current technology and that it will naturally flow through robust relationships and thus help form the organization.

The Process of Improvement

At Chesapeake we have always used a four-step process:

1. Assess the organization/situation.

2. Educate based on what we learned.

3. Have a collaborative design and planning session.

4. Implement the plan and test for results.

Dr. Goldratt, the guru of the Theory of Constraints, says that there are three phases and they are:

- What to Change?
- What to Change To?
- How to Cause the Change?

Assessing an Organization

The first step in assessing any organizational system is to *define* the system, its *purpose,* and how you *measure* attainment of purpose.

When defining the system—are you assessing an entire company, a department within the company, a particular plant, or perhaps a department within a plant? For a consultant, this task should not totally rest on the shoulders of your client, or they may make it either a too narrow focus or too broad. If the focus is too narrow, there is the risk of other areas of the organization having such an impact on the target area that to ignore their impact would render your work useless. If the focus is too large, the system may be so diverse and complex that it would take forever to get anything accomplished.

Also, in assessing the system, is there the realization that there is pain? An old saying in sales is, "No pain, no sale." I think the same thing applies to improvement. If at least a few leaders inside the system do not recognize and feel pain, then any attempt to improve is going to fail. Adults do not make changes unless we think they are necessary. Even when we think they are necessary we may not make them. Unless you are a drill sergeant or equivalent and have the power to inflict massive pain, you will not be able to force people to change.

In our business, we are faced with a variation of the same situation. If someone doesn't act like they really need and want to work with us (not just any old consulting firm but us), then we are wasting time trying to sell them.

During the assessment we need to determine the key process(es) by which an organization creates its value-added proposition. We normally do that by developing process maps through observation and interviews of key personnel. In our assessments we also probe for where the system constraint is and assess if that is a logical place for it to be from a strategic point of view. We once did an assessment for a tier one automotive supplier where they had more than ten million dollars invested in a continuous forging operation. However, the constraint of the system was a chemical wash downstream of the forging machine that cost about fifty thousand dollars. It was an easy decision to spend an additional fifty thousand to double the capacity of wash and insure forging was not blocked by a fifty-thousand-dollar problem.

We also do leadership assessments of key people in the organization. We use the DISC and Values profiles. In addition we use the Personal Talent & Skills Inventory (PTSI) profile. The DISC profile is how someone shows up to work from a behavior point of view. Their values show why they show up, and the PTSI shows how clear they are with respect to internal and external issues, including emotional intelligence.

From the information gathered above, we then design what education and experiences we plan to put folks through.

For example, we did an assessment for a conglomerate that owned two companies that made sucker rods. Sucker rods are used to help extract oil from the ground. The key resource that affected both companies was a particular forging operation in one of the companies that fed both companies' heat treat operations. This forging operation performed very poorly and was way behind on current best manufacturing practices. They also had a very hostile union environment.

The mindset (lack of trust) of the people closest to forging was the constraint of the entire system. This mindset had caused them to act in a manner that was not in alignment with the best interest of the company, including their own well-being. We needed to address this issue or else all efforts would be wasted. This led us to give communications and leadership development education for the workers, supervisors, engineers, and mechanics in forging. This additional step wiped away many erroneous assumptions that people had for one another and opened their minds and hearts for learning new material. We taught them our normal synchronous flow workshops and Lean workshops. We also took them on a field trip to another forging operation that had embraced progressive manufacturing techniques for years. Had we only given them the technical manufacturing training, I doubt we would have made it to first base with these folks. As it was, we ended up with a very nice implementation, and the customer realized a healthy increase in profits.

We are very deliberate in our education using simulators and examples in environments that are not the same as the one within which the client normally works. Otherwise, there is a tendency to think, "Well this will not work in my job because ... " We want them to learn new techniques and approaches in another environment and then transfer that knowledge to their world.

Once the education is complete, we get the carefully selected team to draw their existing processes, show how they work, and explain why they don't give the desired results. We have them use their new knowledge to draw processes that will work for them. After this, they name the obstacles preventing that new system from becoming a reality. They develop action plans to overcome each obstacle and assign responsibilities and time frames. We execute the plan and monitor the work.

It has been our thought to drive the decision making process as far down into the organization as we can. We always see some surprises with respect to people rising to the occasion and showing leadership abilities that, prior to the engagement, no one had recognized. It is one of the things that makes our work very enjoyable.

In one case, we were working two levels down from the plant manager in a large furniture plant. The people we were working with were frontline supervisors and none had a college degree. Within six months of our implementation they were essentially running the facility and getting excellent results. Then something very unusual happened. Due to some inappropriate behavior, the plant manager and all of his direct reports were terminated, leaving the facility without its top two layers of management. With an interim plant manager, those frontline supervisors led the facility to a much higher level of performance. Had that group not been trained and empowered to make change, this transition would not have been possible.

In the implementation phase we are into the topic of change management. Again, so much has been written about this topic that is excellent material that I do not want to spend a lot of time rehashing what others have said. One of the books I think is a must read is *Leading Change* by Kotter. In the book he cites eight things that need to be present:

1. Create a sense of urgency.

2. Create a guiding coalition.

3. Develop a vision and strategy.

4. Communicate the change vision.

5. Empower broad-based action.

6. Generate some short-term wins.

7. Consolidate gains to leverage more change.

8. Anchor new approaches into the culture.

These eight items are a good checklist for leaders to review to see how appropriate they are to their situation and insure they have those bases covered.

Ongoing Improvement

If you take a burning log off the fire, it does not take long for it to lose its heat. The same holds true for improvement. Once one project is done, start another. The way we accomplish this is by creating continuous circuits (just like in an exercise routine) of improvement projects, all of which would include the elements of assess, education, design/plan, and implement. Whatever process of improvement you use, keep it going, otherwise you will experience a spike in performance, a decline, and then a plateau.

Chapter 11

The Evolving Enterprise Leader

When we back up and look at the overall picture, we are looking at connecting two things: 1) the purpose of the organization and 2) growth of the individual leaders/relationships. Both of these are dynamic issues and require some sort of constant attention, or else things start sliding backwards. If we do them well, there are great rewards for you and your team.

I recently visited a long-time client that has engaged in a program to formalize leadership actions for each level in their organization. Desired behavior yields desired results. They had attempted to spell out specifically desired behavior at every level. Had it been anyone other than this particular account I would have written them off as crazy. However, I have enough regard and respect for them that I had to listen intently. I think they are on to something.

My friend, and client, Mark Szpila explained to me that they spent a lot of time pouring over organization, processes, and systems (the way things are done) to insure that these would yield desired results. Then they simply "manage" leader/manager behavior to be in alignment.

They have realized that the pure leadership piece is missing and understand the fact that excellent communications (which again flows through relationships) is very much dependent on leaders knowing themselves and those they are trying to communicate with.

What I think we are learning is that one must continue to grow. We believe the leader as a coach is the next logical step.

Are There Stages of Leadership?

A lot of things happen naturally to form leaders. However, we are addressing an issue where we are proactively trying to improve leadership performance, so we are going to make a stab at some orderly steps and what might be a full-blown leadership agenda.

The first step in becoming a better leader is *self-awareness.* There are a variety of tools that can be used in this step. At Chesapeake, we use DISC as a behavioral assessment that tells an individual *how* they show up everyday. We teach the leader how their style impacts others they are trying to relate to and how they might adapt their behavior for the purpose of better communications with a specific individual or group. We also assess for key motivators, skills, and talents. We follow those assessments up with a coaching call. By the time this process is over, an individual is beginning to get a clearer awareness of who they are and what strengths they bring to the table in order to lead authentically. There are two major advantages of being self-aware: 1) understanding how your particular leadership style may affect others and 2) understanding your own communication blind spots with respect to your ability to listen to others.

The next stage is *role awareness*. What are some of the skills and abilities that a particular role calls for? If the job could talk, what would it want and does the person filling that position have those traits? Normally we have something that an individual can work on to improve their chances of success in a particular role. Role awareness can expand to team mission awareness. What does the team *need* to be successful and do those skill sets exist in the team? This is an exercise of placing the people on your team in the correct position for your company to execute a winning play. For example, if you have three members on a business development team and one is an excellent writer and two are excellent negotiators (all of which can be tested), you want to make sure you are placing them in the proper roles based on their skill sets.

Learning *coaching* and conflict resolution is the logical next state. Coaching may have become one of those fads that started in the nineties and accelerated after the turn of the century. There are tons of executive coaches, and of course, there are organizations that want to train, certify, and give you their stamp of approval to be a coach (all for a hefty price, I might add).

Like all things in leadership, none of these gurus have actually invented anything; the concepts have been around forever.

In a talk to his staff, my good friend and customer Mike Storms told his people that they had four coaching relationships and responsibilities to concern themselves with:

1. Themselves

2. Their peers

3. Their boss

4. Their subordinates

What Mike did was define each person's sphere of influence, which is required to get work done. Again, it is all about relationships. The sphere of influence relationships are a way to focus your improvement.

When should you coach versus direct? Of course, in any emergency, you may want to direct. "Get out of the building because the place is on *fire*," might be a situation where you would not want to use coaching but perhaps a more direct approach.

Note the graph below. At a low skill level and low feeling of ownership, a direct managing approach might be more useful. As the skill level increases and ownership of the issue increases, then more of a coaching approach would be applicable. It is important to note that you, as the leader, can affect someone's progression up that curve. As you teach through letting them think and do, you move them up the curve. What you get out of the whole deal, in addition to satisfaction that you helped someone, is more human capacity to do work. You can either do all the work yourself, or you can partner with those with whom you are connected. It will involve letting go of some control.

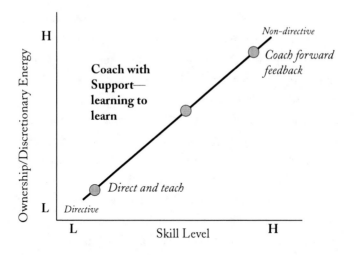

Building Relationships and Responsibility

The leader as a coach is one that is focused on helping people become more confident and competent, which is a mixture of providing a challenge and offering support. It is much more about helping the learner learn versus teaching.

This is a lot tougher than it sounds. It is much easier for your subordinate to dump the problem in your lap for you to solve, and most of the time it is much easier for you to just give the answer. With modern communications technology, we have the ability to do this faster than ever. With a text message, e-mail, or voicemail, you are in the loop of a problem that has not yet approached a solution. With expectation of immediate response, you are tempted to offer your advice. There is another way. That way is to fire the problem back in their direction with some great questions.

Several years ago we gave public workshops throughout the country. Preparation included arranging hotels, food, and other things necessary to pull off an event. I delegated this task to one of our administrative assistants. One morning when I came to work, she hit me with a ton of issues concerning the workshops and wanted me to make the decisions. I said, "Fine. I tell you what. I will go make the decisions on this; however, I was fixing to go back and work on a proposal for an implementation. That means you will have to do that." Wow, you talk about one angry administrative assistant. She went on to make the decisions on the workshops without my input and did an excellent job.

Later that morning, when I figured it was safe to wander near her desk, I said, "Susie (not her real name), I get the feeling that I made you mad this morning." Susie confirmed that I had and she felt that I was an incurable butthead. We had a calm discussion on why I had placed the whole responsibility in her lap and all was well. Now, please don't handle a similar situation like that because I really did cause more tension than needed. Although I could have and should have used a more Socratic approach with Susie, the bottom line is that Susie cannot take her work and dump it in my lap. I already have a boatload of things to do. However, that is exactly what I see happening today in the workplace, especially with more accessible personal communications tools.

Part of successful delegation is positive expectations. You know and believe in your heart that the individual can get the job done successfully. *Successfully* might not mean the way you would do it, but the way they would do it. This falls into the honoring part of leadership. Folks will perform to your minimum expectations so you, as the leader, must constantly lift those expectations and thoughts to a higher level. I actually put folks I work with on my prayer list and really try and lift them up. Those elevated expectations can be transformational.

Part of honoring someone in a coaching relationship is *Being*:

- Be interested in what they are doing to the point of asking deeper questions.

- Accept who they are as an individual and do not let it bias your thoughts of what they may come up with.

- Give them your support and encouragement.

- Laser focus on what the end result needs to look like and paint that picture together so it is common to you and your team.

In order to do this successfully, some of the skills you must *Have* and hone are:

- The ability to ask some thought-provoking questions. Remember your goal is to help them learn, not to teach. "What in the heck caused that to happen?"

- The ability to listen beyond the words and the courage to probe deeper. "Hmm, that is interesting. Tell me more."

- The ability to formulate a decent action plan and ask for a commitment and timetable for the plan. There needs to always be a next step in the process. "What would be a good time for us to get back together?"

- The ability to encourage them to overcome obstacles and help them gain confidence in their ability. "I feel good about your special skills to make this happen." (If they do not stand a snowball's chance in an oven, then don't give them the project).

Asking great questions is one of the best ways a leader/coach can be *Disruptive*. Someone once taught me that the best questions for coaching are "what" questions. Here are some great what questions:

1. What is going well?

2. What support do you need?

3. If this challenge was solved, what would it open up for you?

4. What is really getting in the way?

5. What could be the first step?

6. What would be the easiest way to do this?

7. What are you truly passionate about?

8. What is the worst thing that could happen? (That is a great one for getting people to do something about which they are uncomfortable.)

9. What concerns you about this strategy?

10. What do you want to focus our time on today so that when you leave you will be able to say "this was worth it"?

11. What do you need for me to do?

One of the final steps in a leadership/coach encounter is *Aligning.* We want to insure we have recapped the conversation and included the identification of the issue, what we learned, our plan moving forward, and what obstacles we have to overcome.

If we are able to stay disciplined and adhere to this process, not only will we be more effective in the short run, but we will also build leaders for tomorrow. Disciples make more disciples and leaders make more leaders.

Chapter 12

Manufacturing Leaders

It is a tad scary, but I am pushing forty years of experience in manufacturing. I do not see writing too many more business books, so I wanted to write a special chapter on manufacturing. Enterprise Fitness is a concept that can be used in any organization, and all that we said in the previous eleven chapters also applies to any manufacturing facility.

I want to focus these discussions on manufacturing leadership, such as plant managers and vice presidents of operations.

I started my career in the chemical process industry and worked for DuPont and Stauffer Chemicals. I can recall a plant manager at DuPont was almost like a god. Our plant manager seemed like he was old as Methuselah, wore a coat and tie to work, and had the highest level of respect. We even had an assistant plant manager who was just a couple of notches lower than a god. To become a plant manager was like being the captain of your own ship, and the assistant plant manager was like an executive officer. It was a high honor and with that came a lot of respect, authority, and responsibility. These are the people that probably were the best engineers, the best area managers, superintendents, etc. They had earned their position. Along the way, they were mentored in the DuPont way, and by the time they reached the position of plant manager they were very well qualified to execute their duties as the head of a large plant with huge capital and human resources.

It seemed operations executives were well equipped for the job. The larger companies had capacity to invest in people, so a young engineer (and most plant managers initially started out in engineering) went through many experiences over a ten to fifteen year period that would prepare them for increased responsibility. In fact, the large companies not only supplied leadership for themselves but also found many of their young folks moving on to other companies, taking advantage of the excellent training they had received. I was one of those and ended up managing my first plant before I was thirty.

With nearly thirty years of downsizing, right sizing, and all other sorts of sizing, the capacity to mentor and teach people has been radically reduced. This hit home to me several years ago when I visited the factory of a Fortune 500 Company. The place was an absolute mess, and the poor plant manager was totally clueless as to what was going on and what to do first. His staff was even more clueless. The young plant manager was not stupid; he had just never been taught or mentored.

Why Are We Here?

Everyone in the facility needs to understand why the plant exists. When I took over the Sherwin-Williams facility in

Baltimore, I wanted everyone to know that the only reason we existed was to supply product to our customers. We made paint and adhesives for people who had a need and were willing to pay us money. Everyone, including accounting, maintenance, and human resources, needed to be locked into that goal.

I recently attended a change of command ceremony for the Coast Guard Yard at Curtis Bay near Baltimore. Our neighbor, Captain John Kaplan, was taking over command and had invited Linda and me. In his speech, John explained to the Yard why they existed, "We fix ships." Pretty clear. They take ships that are broken and transform them into ships that are not broken.

In order to fulfill the mission of making something, we need to:

1. Provide a safe and healthy work environment.

2. Produce a good quality product that meets our customers' requirements.

3. Deliver the product on time and have a competitive lead time.

4. Be productive and cost competitive.

5. Provide a fun place to work.

6. Comply with all government laws and regulations.

I think a mindset that we may have lost over the last several decades is the mindset of accountability. The plant manager needs to be accountable and take charge over the above issues. A plant manager cannot offload or delegate safety to human resources or some other staff function. Although there are staff functions that address almost all of the above categories, the plant manager needs to understand that they are the ones accountable and, therefore, must understand and assert what influence is necessary to insure the job is accomplished correctly.

Earlier in the book I said some unkind things about Sherwin-Williams and Jack Breen, their CEO. I will give Mr. Breen credit for one thing, he did give authority along with responsibility. As a plant manager, I had complete control of everything I needed. One time I was having quality problems with our latex supplier. Purchasing out of Cleveland had negotiated this super deal with the vendor, but the vendor was not providing good product and was going to affect my plants' results. Much to the protest and chagrin of corporate purchasing, I changed suppliers. It was one of the few times I had to flex my plant manager muscles, but it underscored the authority/responsibility bond because no one group was as powerful as corporate purchasing.

Safety

DuPont used to say that safety was *equal* to production, quality, cost, and morale. Some get all emotional and say it is more important, and I would have probably been in that camp until I pondered the logic. The safest thing to do is stay home in bed, so it can't be the most important—it is equal. As an aside, DuPont did have data indicating that you were safer in one of their plants than you were at home.

From a morale standpoint, we must provide a safe and healthy place for people to work. The proper thought process is:

1. We do not jeopardize someone's safety or health for any reason.

2. We do not jeopardize quality for production or cost.

3. We do not jeopardize service for cost.

I am going to lean heavily on my DuPont training, since they were the trailblazers with regard to safety in industry. This stemmed from a family member being killed in an industrial explosion and a vow by the family to excel in safety.

You must believe that all accidents can be prevented. Over ninety-six percent of all accidents are caused by unsafe acts and unsafe conditions. Unsafe acts and unsafe conditions are caused by attitude, and attitude can be changed. You as the plant manager must carry this torch, set the example, and lead the program.

If you do not already have an attitude-based safety program, go get one. DuPont's STOP program is one, but there are plenty more on the market that I am sure are just as effective.

Each department/plant should have some sort of a monthly safety meeting and topic. If you have a workmen's compensation insurance company, they are a wonderful resource for films and material. This is an area where your HR department can support you.

Here are some other quick hitters to consider in your overall safety program:

- Fork truck training. A fork truck is one of the most dangerous pieces of equipment roaming your plant.

- Lock and tag procedures such as "lock-tag-and-try."

- Good housekeeping. Your Lean 5S program could be considered part of your safety program. Once you get the place really cleaned up, take some pictures and have them posted throughout the facility as a reminder to everyone what it should look like for the next oncoming shift.

- Personal protective equipment. I think safety glasses are mandatory in every plant and hard hats in most. One of the things that personal protective equipment does is set a tone for someone. When I don this hard hat and walk through these doors, I just clicked into a different more aware gear.

- Emergency drills.

- Off the job safety programs.

- Celebrations, award lunches, and prizes for achieving goals.

I have found when putting in a new, progressive safety program that some of the old guard will test you. There will come a situation where one of your subordinates presents a scenario where it is, "We either service our best customer or we can be safe." It may not be in those exact words, but the challenge will come. Your response is to embrace the beauty of the and. You are going to do both—serve our best customer *and* do it safely.

In my career, if I had to point to one thing that gives me the most pleasure, it is to look back at those facilities that went from people getting hurt to no one getting hurt, and each of those plants ended up at a much higher level of productivity.

John Covington

We have talked about safety from a morale perspective. It is also an economic issue. Safe plants are more productive and profitable plants. The insurance savings alone can be huge for a plant that has little risk of injury.

Quality

At its basic level, we must meet customer specifications so they will be satisfied with our product. At the bare minimum our quality program needs to insure we are shipping good stuff.

Quality is another area I have seen moved outside of operations with the statement, "We do not want the fox guarding the hen house." Statements like that make the blood of any operations person boil. It does mine. The inference is that operations people have no problem shipping garbage as long as they hit their production numbers. Again, as plant manager, regardless of where quality reports, you are responsible. It is also important to note that improved quality means improved productivity.

In my career I have seen a lot of different quality initiatives going back to Deming, Juran, Crosby, the Quality Circle craze, Baldridge Award hype, ISO 9000, and now Six Sigma. Unfortunately this is where I feel fads and slogans began to creep into manufacturing to replace real people that knew the science of making things in mass.

GE is one of the proponents of Six Sigma. Linda and I have a GE dishwasher. The darn thing has had four recalls on it, and each one somehow ends up costing us money. Someone definitely failed to six sigma our dishwasher. It is scary that the same people that made my dishwasher also produce jet engines for aircraft.

You have to have a quality program as part of your culture of ongoing improvement. I think many of the abovementioned fads/programs are too complicated and become goals unto themselves. We have clients that count the number of black and green belts they have. Who cares? I have not yet seen the correlation between number of black belts and improved quality. It sure did not work for GE.

I recommend going simple. I had enormous success at two facilities (including Sherwin-Williams) by just implementing the simple Quality Circle program. This program taught the basics of quality including data collection, different graphs, and simple statistical analysis and problem solving. Another advantage of the Quality Circle program is that it engaged the direct line workers in not only quality issues but business acumen. Every quality program I have seen says almost exactly the same thing and uses exactly the same tools. I would go with the one that is the easiest to implement and least costly.

Quality, like safety, is another area where your leadership may be tested. I have found quality to not be as clear cut as safety and health issues. Many times our self-imposed specs are unreasonable with respect to what the customer wants/needs. I recall one time I was filtering paint through a 10 micron filter, because that is what our internal spec required. It was taking forever, so the salesmen came into the plant to see what was going on. When he saw we were filtering it through a 10 micron, he almost passed out from high blood pressure. After his initial flurry of cuss words, I finally understood, "Hey John, this paint goes in a dip tank where bark, cats, acorns, and other garbage will fall. Filter the paint through a potato sack and lets get this thing shipped." So, do you be stupid and continue to filter through a 10 micron or ship the product? Good question for you to ponder, and how would you handle that situation?

You must not ship anything that you know is not going to meet customer satisfaction/requirements. Like safety, improving quality performance translates to improved cost performance.

Production/Service

This is the area where we get into issues of flow, cycle time, due date performance, inventory control, supply chain, and everything else that deals with transforming raw material into a product ready to ship.

When you flow something, there are only four elements to consider:

1. Dependency
2. Issues of capacity
3. Inventory
4. Variability

Your mission as a plant is to quickly and smoothly move material and work through the various resources of the plant in concert with market demand.

As the plant manager or VP of operations, you need to understand how your product flows. What are the key constraints in your processes and what is your overall capacity? The capacity of your plant is the capacity of the constraint in the system. In continuous chemical process plants, that constraint is normally quite obvious.

It has been my experience that most people do not know squat about flow and have not seen the need to spend time learning. I would encourage you to learn the basics about flow through systems then apply that learning to your facilities. There are several excellent books written on the topic of synchronized manufacturing by Dr. Mike Umble. I would start there and perhaps attend some workshops on synchronized manufacturing. This subject matter is deep and gets into various plant configurations, MRP, and other scheduling systems.

Productivity and Cost

Actually, if you perform well on the top three areas of safety, quality, and service, the cost and productivity numbers should fall into place. On bonus plans that I put in, I would normally wave the cost segment of the plan if all of the other areas were hitting target. My reason for doing that is that I did not want my employees focusing on cost because that would take their focus off everything else. Besides, there is very little you can do about costs, since most of them are fixed by the time you get to the operations level. I know I may catch some grief for that statement, but I believe it to be true in many cases.

Going through an exercise in Lean Thinking is always a good idea to expose and remove waste. Lean Thinking is another area where there is plenty of literature, and I would encourage any manufacturing executive to be familiar with and embrace the principles.

This is where I get a little uneasy because as the head of operations, many times you have little or no input how you are measured with regard to productivity and cost. Variance to standard cost, adherence to budget, and units per labor hour are all possible measures of cost/productivity. I actually disagree with all of those.

"Show me how you measure me, and I will show you how I behave. If you measure me in a stupid manner, do not complain when I act stupid."

I think I can best describe some productivity and cost issues by a few examples from my Sherwin-Williams days. I took over a plant in 1985 that was behind on everything, and every area of endeavor was amiss. Safety was awful, quality was poor, we were behind on orders, costs were out of control, morale was terrible, and we were not in compliance with many environmental laws. Other than that the facility was doing pretty well.

I focused on unified purpose (we make paint and adhesives for our customers), safety, quality, and service. It is obvious how improved safety and quality performance improved productivity and cost. Let's talk about flow.

The constraint of our commercial paint plant was grinding. The most that facility could possibly make without additional capital was the amount we could squeeze through the grinding operation, so that is where we focused attention—like a laser. What we found was that grinding was running only about sixty percent of the time for a variety of reasons. One reason was that the area was understaffed as a result of years of cost cutting mentality. There was one operator per shift per machine, and that operator was expected to do everything—do set ups, take samples to the lab, clean up the area, etc. Many of those functions were not direct running of the grinding operation, thus the machine was essentially down. I doubled the head count in grinding (did not get permission but figured I would get forgiveness). By doubling the head count and some other smaller items, we were able to increase volume through grinding by twenty-five percent. What this means is that volume through the entire complex increased by twenty-five percent, and all of that paint was sold. It was a huge positive impact to the bottom line, and cost per gallon went way down because of the increased gallons. Doubling the budgeted head count in the area may have seemed counter intuitive, but when done at the system's constraint it makes sense.

There are two reasons for measures:

1.   External reporting
2.   Internal control

They do not have to be the same measurement system.

The Lean movement has also discovered that traditional ways of measuring a manufacturing operation are in conflict with good Lean practices.

Operating expense is a function of the general characteristics of your flow system. If you do not change your general characteristics, you will not be able to make an appreciable difference in the amount of money you spend to produce product. This is where programs like Lean thinking can make an impact. When you initiate Lean projects, you are changing the flow system to eliminate waste and unnecessary work.

For measures of productivity, I am biased toward value added (sales less truly variable cost—raw materials and outside processing) divided by operating expense.

Here is a great piece of advice—determine your value added per constraint unit for each product. I bet you will find some surprises. Many times through selling price you can force the most economical product mix through your facility, and the value added per constraint unit is the best way to do it.

Provide a Fun Place to Work

This is back to that relationship thing. You cannot manage a plant from your office. You have to get out and engage people. This is where that *honoring* thing comes into your game plan. Honor your folks. Respect who they are, love them, and help them get better.

Do not assume that people understand what you said. In fact, assume that they do not understand what you said and over-communicate. This can be difficult for folks that struggle with being outgoing. Many operations executives are of the personality type that trust their own intuition over others. That is okay—that just means you need to work harder at that communication thing.

Comply with the Law

This is a category that I added recently. There are so many new laws and regulations concerning labor, environmental safety, and other areas for people that run facilities that it is almost over-whelming. I think this is where HR staffers can be a big help. Operations executives need someone to stay on top of what all needs to be done. Again, you as the leader are responsible.

Under most of these areas there are specific numbers to hit. These numbers are a great foundation for your bonus plan. My recommendation is to make the entire team respon-sible for the exact same numbers. They may initially hate you for that, but they will have to work with one another as a team to win. That is a good thing.

In annual planning you can develop goals and specific projects to improve each one of the areas that lead to a well run manufacturing facility.

Chapter 13

Creating a Fit Enterprise

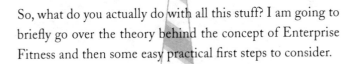

So, what do you actually do with all this stuff? I am going to briefly go over the theory behind the concept of Enterprise Fitness and then some easy practical first steps to consider.

Brief Theory Summary

I like the vision of the farmer (the leader) tending to the soil (the culture) in order to improve the yield of fruit (the purpose for the system) to begin our summary discussion.

What we want is more and better fruit year after year. We know the leader must address the culture to get more crops. There are many, many agricultural analogies in the Bible. Perhaps all living things have similar patterns, and we can learn by looking and learning from those agricultural cycles. It has been my experience that human systems behave exactly the same as any other system in nature, so we can learn a lot just by observing things like nature and agriculture.

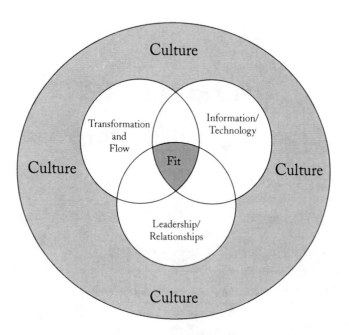

In human systems, culture is comprised of purpose, relationships, and information. In Enterprise Fitness we restated these elements to make them more compatible with business organizations. We call purpose Transformation and Flow (T&F), because all organizations transform something from one state of being to another. T&F includes the processes that must be in place to achieve the transformation. In our culture model, we add leadership to relationship. We also added technology to information. I will emphasize again that information flows through relationships. The better and more robust the relationships, the better and more robust the information flow.

For a fit enterprise, we want to focus on the area where all of these three overlap and are one since that is where culture arises.

John Covington

The leader (farmer) is key. Imagine the Enterprise Leadership Model embedded inside the "fit" in the culture model. What the individuals *Do* critically impacts the whole thing and we know that *Do* is held up by *Be, Have,* and *Renew.*

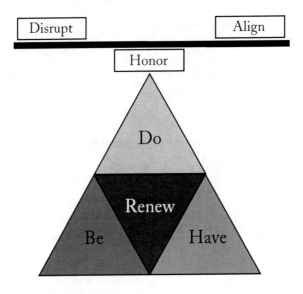

Action Summary

Here are some suggested steps:

1. Do an assessment of the transformation and flow part of your organization. What is the purpose, how do you measure it, and how are you doing? If the church can measure disciples, then you can measure progress relative to your purpose. I have yet to see an organization that cannot be measured. Define the processes involved in your transformation and flow and what the constraint resource is.

2. Assess the leadership team. We use a variety of assessments tools that address behavior, values, skill, and current leadership expertise. Personal interviews should be part of this assessment.

3. Design an improvement plan based on what was learned in the assessment of leadership and T&F.

4. Make necessary changes with respect to process and people. I do not think I have ever seen a successful implementation where both of these areas did not undergo some change.

5. Continue to implement and monitor results.

6. Go back to step one and start over.

I had a young business owner ask me one time, "John, when does all this chaos end?" I answered, "When you die, so enjoy the journey."

Appendix

For years I have been drawn to 1 Corinthians chapters 12 and 13 as a wonderful model of organizational systems and how they should operate. Close your eyes and imagine that high school chemistry model again. It is the one with the different size and different colored spheres attached by varying sizes of rods. Imagine the spheres as people and the rods as the relationship between people—some rods are short and thick, indicating a close relationship (bond), and others are thin and long. Now, imagine the model in three dimensional motion and spheres breaking off and leaving the molecule and others coming in and being attached. Of course this represents people leaving and joining the organization. See the connection of this molecule with others.

Now read these two chapters. Consider that chapter 12 represents an organization with a common purpose. In chapter 12 Paul is describing the church as the body of Christ. Note the need for different types of talents (that are held by people) and that only together do they make something significant. Chapter 12 is an amazing depiction of any organization.

Chapter 13 addresses the bond between two spheres that

we will call the relationship. Chapter 13 discusses how that relationship should be. I picked the contemporary English version for these chapters because for many it is easier to understand. Read, enjoy, and discern.

1 Corinthians 12:4–26

There are different kinds of spiritual gifts, but they all come from the same Spirit. There are different ways to serve the same Lord, and we can each do different things. Yet the same God works in all of us and helps us in everything we do. The Spirit has given each of us a special way of serving others. Some of us can speak with wisdom, while others can speak with knowledge, but these gifts come from the same Spirit. To others the Spirit has given great faith of the power to heal the sick or the power to work mighty miracles. Some of us are prophets, and some of us recognize when God's Spirit is present. Others can speak different kinds of languages, and still others can tell what these languages mean. But it is the Spirit who does all this and decides which gifts to give to each of us.

The body of Christ has many different parts, just as any other body does. Some of us are Jews, and others are Gentiles. Some of us are slaves, and others are free. But God's Spirit baptized each of us and made us part of the body of Christ. Now we each drink from that same Spirit.

Our bodies don't have just one part. They have many parts. Suppose a foot says, "I'm not a hand, and so I'm not part of the body." Wouldn't the foot still belong to the body? Or suppose an ear says, "I'm not an eye, and so I'm not part of the body." Wouldn't the ear still belong to the body? If our bodies were only an eye, we couldn't hear a thing. But God has put all parts of our body together in the way that he decided is best.

A body isn't really a body, unless there is more than one part. It takes many parts to make a single body. That's why the eyes cannot say they don't need hands. That's also why the head cannot say it doesn't need the feet. In fact, we cannot get along without the parts of the body that seem to be the weakest. We take special care to dress up some parts of our bodies. We are modest about our personal parts, but we don't have to be modest about other parts. God put our bodies together in such a way that even the parts that seem the least important are valuable.

He did this to make all parts of the body work together smoothly, with each part caring about the others. If one part of our body hurts, we hurt all over. If one part of our body is honored, the whole body will be happy.

1 Corinthians 13

What if I could speak all languages of humans and of angels? If I did not love others I would be nothing more than a noisy gong or a clanging cymbal. What if I could prophesy and understand all secrets and all knowledge? And what if I had faith that moved mountains? I would be nothing, unless I loved others. What if I gave away all that I owned and let myself be burned alive? I would gain nothing, unless I loved others. Love is kind and patient, never jealous, boastful, proud, or rude. Love isn't selfish or quick tempered. It doesn't keep a record of wrongs that others do. Love rejoices in the truth, but not in evil. Love is always supportive, loyal, hopeful, and trusting. Love never fails.

Everyone who prophesies will stop, and unknown languages will no longer be spoken. All that we know will be forgotten. We don't know everything, and our prophecies are not complete. But what is perfect will someday appear, and what isn't perfect will then disappear.

When we were children we thought and reasoned as children do. But when we grew up, we quit our childish ways. Now all we can see of God is like a cloudy picture in a mirror. Later we will see him face to face. We don't know everything, but then we will, just as God completely understands us. For now there are faith, hope, and love. But of these three, the greatest is love.